How to
Deal With Parents Who Are
Angry,
Troubled,
Afraid, or
Just
Plain Crazy

CORWIN
PRESS

The Corwin Press logo—a raven striding across an open book—represents the happy union of courage and learning. We are a professional-level publisher of books and journals for K–12 educators, and we are committed to creating and providing resources that embody these qualities. Corwin's motto is "Success for All Learners."

Elaine K. McEwan

How to
Deal With Parents
Who Are
Angry,
Troubled,
Afraid, or
Just
Plain Crazy

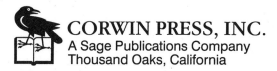

CORWIN PRESS, INC.
A Sage Publications Company
Thousand Oaks, California

For information:

Corwin Press, Inc.
A Sage Publications Company
2455 Teller Road
Thousand Oaks, California 91320
E-mail: order@corwinpress.com

SAGE Publications Ltd.
6 Bonhill Street
London EC2A 4PU
United Kingdom

SAGE Publications India Pvt. Ltd.
M-32 Market
Greater Kailash I
New Delhi 110 048 India

Printed in the United States of America

Library of Congress Cataloging-in-Publication Data

McEwan, Elaine K., 1941-
    How to deal with parents who are angry, troubled, afraid, or just plain crazy/by Elaine K. McEwan.
        p. cm.
    Includes bibliographical references and index.
    ISBN 0-8039-6524-9 (cloth: acid-free paper).
    —ISBN 0-8039-6525-7 (pbk.: acid-free paper)
    1. Home and school—United States. 2. Education—Parent participation—United States. 3. Parents—United States—Psychology. I. Title.
    LC225.3.M395   1998
    371.9'2'0973—dc21   97-45277

This book is printed on acid-free paper.

00 01 02 03 10 9 8 7 6 5 4

Production Editor: Michèle Lingre
Production Assistant: Denise Santoyo
Editorial Assistant: Kristen L. Gibson
Typesetter/Designer: Marion Warren
Cover Designer: Marcia M. Rosenburg

CONTENTS

About the Author

Elaine K. McEwan is an educational consultant with the McEwan-Adkins Group, which offers training for school districts in leadership and team building, writing workshops for children, and parenting seminars. A former teacher, librarian, principal, and assistant superintendent for instruction in a suburban Chicago school district, she is the author of over two dozen books, including titles for parents and teachers (*Attention Deficit Disorder*), fiction for middle-grade students (*Joshua McIntire Series*), and guides for administrators (*Leading Your Team to Excellence: How to Make Quality Decisions*). She is the education columnist for the *Oro Valley Explorer* (Arizona) newspaper, a contributing editor to several parenting magazines on educational issues, and can be heard on a variety of syndicated radio programs helping parents solve schooling problems.

She was honored by the Illinois Principals Association as an outstanding instructional leader, by the Illinois State Board of Education with an Award of Excellence in the Those Who Excel Program, and by the National Association of Elementary School Principals as the National Distinguished Principal from Illinois for 1991.

She received her undergraduate degree in education from Wheaton College and graduate degrees in library science and educational administration from Northern Illinois University.

McEwan lives with her husband and business partner, E. Raymond Adkins, in Oro Valley, Arizona.

Introduction

In the fall of 1983, I was hired for my first principalship at an elementary school in a far western suburb of Chicago. Armed with a newly acquired doctoral degree in administration and "dressed for success," I eagerly anticipated helping teachers improve their instructional effectiveness, setting high expectations for students, and developing curriculum. Somewhere along the way, I must have missed the course to prepare me for the almost daily encounters I would have with parents who were angry, troubled, afraid, or in some cases, just plain crazy. Although the latter group was certainly a small minority, there were enough parents in my school (and I'm sure yours is no different) who seemed to leave all reason and common sense at the front door as they stormed the office. Dealing with these moms and dads often made me feel like I was picking my way through a minefield, ignorant of where the next explosion would occur.

Oh, I'd had the requisite school-community relations course. But the syllabus contained nothing about marriage and family counseling or conflict resolution. I started to think that perhaps I'd earned the wrong degree, but it was too late. The problems were on my doorstep from day one. I remember one incident in Technicolor. It was Halloween, and the excitement in the hallways was palpable. A parade headlined the afternoon's festivities, and I had my costume hung on the back of the office door. I would change at lunch time.

My secretary pronounced my Busy Bee getup perfect. "Great choice. You're always buzzing around," she said. I was too distracted to reflect on exactly what she meant and headed to the hallway as the children came in from lunch recess. I was greeted with compliments and calls of delight. My black leotards and turtleneck were topped with an oversized garbage bag of the same color, striped with wide yellow tape. Tightly secured at my arms, legs, and neck, the bag made a perfect bee body. The pièce de résistance of my costume was a headpiece on which golden spheres bobbed from springy wires.

After 2 months on the job, I was feeling confident, and I looked forward to greeting the many parents who traditionally attended the parade. My euphoria lasted all of 15 seconds before I was blindsided by a mom I'd already come to know and love. She sailed into the office with eyes blazing. Fortunately, she was armed with nothing but her tongue, but it proceeded to deliver a lashing that could have bested any belt or razor strop. "No one is going to treat my child like that," she screamed. "Do something." I longed for a genie to appear and calm this crazed woman, but no one came to my rescue. I took her into my office and elicited the story. She just happened to be walking down the hall when her third-grade daughter's class went by on its way to the rest rooms. Naturally, the classroom teacher selected this precise moment to give the aforementioned daughter a good dressing down for all the world to see and hear, including mom. An unfortunate juxtaposition of circumstances, to be sure. I wished at that moment for an alien spaceship to land on the playground and transport teacher, child, and parent to outer space. They were all out of control. What was I to do? Desperate for any solution, I suggested a meeting after school with the teacher. Mom insisted that her husband, who was only a phone call away, come immediately to school and talk with me. Apparently, she felt that he could put me in my place. He arrived shortly, gave me the once-over in my bee costume, and slumped into a corner in my office, saying nothing. Obviously, he'd learned that it was best to be seen and not heard. Dressed in camouflage that obviously wasn't part of a Halloween costume, I expected he might pull a gun from beneath his jacket at any moment.

Once again, mom recounted the story of her daughter's humiliation in vivid detail. The retelling only fueled her anger, and she demanded that I fire the teacher on the spot. Save for tenure, it was a tempting thought. Still no word from dad. We agreed that we would meet with the teacher after school to gather more information; dad nodded his assent. He eyeballed me head to toe one last time and quietly followed his wife from the office.

As soon as the parade ended, I made a quick change out of my costume, raced to the third-grade hallway, and briefed the teacher on my tentative plan for the meeting. "Stay calm, listen, and then be prepared to apologize for losing your cool in front of the world," I advised. "Above all, don't be defensive or raise your voice." I was grateful it was Friday, and I'd have the weekend to recover.

The meeting went as well as could be expected. We all agreed that the daughter's behavior was unacceptable. We all agreed (even the teacher) that the teacher's behavior was unacceptable. I even coaxed a small apology out of mom for being so disruptive and inappropriate earlier. Still no word from dad. He seemed content to watch from the sidelines. It was nearly 5:00 p.m. when everyone filed out of my office. Dad brought up the rear. Just before we reached the door, he leaned over and whispered something in my ear. "I liked you better in your bee costume," he said with a wink. A sexist remark to be sure, but for me, it was the perfect ending to a "no good, very bad, horrible day" in the life of an average principal.

In the years that followed, my meetings with parents who were angry, troubled, afraid, or just plain crazy would become commonplace. I no longer developed sweaty palms, a racing heart, and blotchy skin. I became a confident and capable administrator who had acquired the skills to calm the angriest and to counsel the most troubled.

In the pages ahead, I'll share the strategies that have helped me deal with parents who were out of control. You'll learn how to emerge unscathed from those "close encounters of the parental kind," and you'll even find yourself enjoying the satisfaction that comes from finding solutions to difficult problems. Chapter 1 describes the parents of today's children and discusses the critical issues that cause misunderstandings in schools. Chapter 2 includes dozens of strategies for defusing parents who are angry, troubled, afraid, or just plain crazy. Chapter 3 sets forth a foolproof problem-solving process you can use in any situation. Chapter 4 is titled "Promoting a Healthy School: How to Tell If Your School Is Sick and How to Make It Well." After reading this chapter, you'll be able to analyze your school environment to discover whether you and your faculty are unwittingly encouraging unhealthy communication and a dysfunctional "school family." Last, Chapter 5 includes dozens of proactive things you can do to develop a supportive and involved parent community.

1

Why So Many Parents Are Angry, Troubled, Afraid, or Just Plain Crazy

> Seek first to understand, before you seek to be understood.
>
> —Stephen Covey (1989, p. 235)

> Managing a difficult person means first managing oneself.
>
> —Carol Tavris (1989, p. 295)

There's a lot of questioning, blaming, and downright hostility out there. And it's going both ways. Parents aren't as willing as they used to be to support the schools, either philosophically or financially, and educators are getting more vocal about parents' shortcomings as well. Parents are resentful of what they perceive to be an anti-achievement ideology in today's schools (Leo, 1997; Mack, 1997), and educators and social transformationists point to absentee parents who, more concerned with promotions than parenting, seem to need a strong dose of supervision and accountability themselves. The ultimate losers in this somewhat scary scenario are the kids. But while the ideologues and policymakers are trying to figure out just who is to blame for the public's disenchantment with one of its most pervasive institutions and how to reverse this disturbing trend (Matthews, 1996), administrators and teachers in individual schools are left to handle the fallout—parents who are angry, troubled, afraid, or just plain crazy.

I've personally experienced school problems from both sides of the desk. I've been mad, distressed, and scared. I can also think of at least one occasion when my daughter's principal probably muttered, "That woman is crazy," under her breath as I left the office steaming over an unresolved problem. I know how parents feel when they have a problem and find that no one is willing to address it. As an administrator, I've also encountered my share of parents whose overwrought emotions stood in the way of seeing issues clearly and addressing problems squarely. Educators cannot afford to ignore upset parents, for when moms and dads are unhappy with the schools (and the people who run them), their kids pay the price. One of our key responsibilities as instructional leaders is to maintain positive attitudes toward students, staff, and parents to ensure that all children can learn. This includes "demonstrating concern and openness in the consideration of student, teacher, and/or parent problems and participating in the resolution of such problems where appropriate" and "modeling appropriate human relations skills" (McEwan, 1997b, p. 129). We are the frontline interpreters of educational policy. We are responsible for the quality and effectiveness of classroom teachers. We are "accountable for fostering the kind of school climate where the dignity and worth of all individuals without regard to appearance, race, creed, sex, ability or disability, or social status is of paramount importance" (McEwan, 1997b, p. 133).

Although dozens of distressed and disturbed parents may walk into your office, few should leave feeling the same way. Will they always get what they want? No. Will you always agree with them? Of course not. But should you listen carefully to everything they have to say and engage in meaningful problem solving with them? Always. It's easy to be gracious and warm to a parent who is positive and cooperative, but how do you handle many of today's parents, those who question and accuse? First of all, try to understand why they feel the way they do. In many cases, it's with good reason. I must warn you that you may be tempted to close this book in frustration before you finish this chapter. The litany of scenarios that disturb parents can make for depressing reading. But even when you're not responsible for their feelings, you have to deal with them, and how better to do that than armed with information and understanding?

What Are the Parents of Today Like?

Gone are the "good old days" when principals (and other educators) were revered and respected for their wisdom and position by parents. Now, we have to earn our respect the old-fashioned way: Work for it. And it's a daily assignment. Today's parents are a different breed—less trusting of our educational platitudes and quick to attack what they perceive to be stupidity, inconsistency, stonewalling, or incompetence in the public schools. They don't want us to do things without good reasons, and they resent being told to "just trust us." Here's a small sample of the kinds of parents you may find waiting in your office on any given day.

Parents Who Are Less Respectful of Authority

This lack of respect shows up everywhere—in their exchanges with teachers, in public meetings, and especially in how they treat administrators. Angry exchanges at school board meetings are commonplace, and courtesies that once were taken for granted are now unusual and noteworthy. Dealing with parents who lack respect for us means that before we can move to problem solving, we must first establish rapport.

*Parents Who Are More Educated About Schools and
View Schools as One More Service to Be "Consumed"*

Check out the shelves of your public library, and you will find dozens of volumes written to give parents the inside track on choosing the best schools and teachers for their children, titles such as *School Savvy: Everything You Need to Know to Guide Your Child Through Today's Schools* (Harrington & Young, 1993) and *How to Get Your Child a Private School Education in a Public School* (Nemko & Nemko, 1986). In *Getting the Best Education for Your Child,* James Keogh (1996, p. 25) offers these suggestions to parents about how to lobby assertively for their child's education:

- Don't be intimidated by your child's teacher.
- Don't be afraid of the doctor [administrator].
- Bring the bosses down to size.

- Read your teachers' contracts.
- Don't be too trusting.

The aforementioned books treat school issues generically, but in communities around the country, parents and publishers are also bringing out ratings booklets for local schools that contain test scores, descriptive information, and even statistical analyses about school effectiveness (Bradley, 1997, pp. 33-34).

Parents Who Are Cynical and Distrustful

Today's parents are a reflection of our society at large, unwilling to trust institutions that have taken their trust and misused it. They don't believe it just because we say so. They want to see budgets, curricula, test scores, and research. They question our judgment, quibble with our reasons, and demand more information than they ever wanted in the past. In their book, *How to Deal with Community Criticism of School Change*, Ledell and Arnsparger (1993, pp. v-vi) offer a variety of suggestions for how to prepare in advance for restructuring and reform efforts in a school or district. But most telling is a checklist in the introduction designed to help the reader determine if he or she actually needs the book. The authors advise buying the book if *

- More and more people in your community are expressing concerns about programs, projects, and other initiatives to improve student learning.
- School board meetings are drawing more people complaining about the curriculum, instruction, testing, health education, or objectionable books.
- Teachers are receiving more requests to exempt students from attending certain classes or from reading specific curriculum materials.
- School and central administration staff are spending significantly more time on the phone or meeting with people who have concerns about the school.

NOTE: Excerpts from *How to Deal With Community Criticism of School Change* published by the Education Commission of the States (ECS), 707 17th Street, Suite 2700, Denver, CO 80202-3427, (303) 299-3600. © 1993, ECS. All rights reserved. Reprinted with permission.

Parents Who Are Activists

The parents of today just don't sit around and talk; they get organized. Leah Vukmir of Wauwatosa, Wisconsin, organized PRESS (Parents Raising Educational Standards in Schools), a 1,000-member organization pressing for changes in the classroom (http://www.execp.com//pressiws/). Mary Damer (personal communication, July 13, 1997) was so upset with the direction her Illinois school district was taking that she founded Taxpayers for Academic Priorities in St. Charles Schools. The Education Consumers Clearinghouse Network, headquartered at East Tennessee State University in Johnson City, coordinates an electronic network of activist parent groups around the country (http://www.tricon.net/Comm/educon). As an administrator in today's schools, be ready for parent involvement that is far more sophisticated than providing cupcakes and cookies for the annual bake sale.

Parents Who Are Increasingly Disengaged
From the Public School

At the opposite end of the involvement continuum are parents who don't care about the public schools anymore. They are home schooling or enrolling their children in private options. In his book, *Is There a Public for the Public Schools?*, David Matthews (1996) writes that the public has become deeply ambivalent about the role of public schools. People want to support them but also want their children to receive a good education, and, increasingly, they see the two goals as conflicting.

Parents Who Are Feeling Stressed and Guilty

Many of today's parents lead very complicated lives replete with daily planners, cell phones, and nannies. They rarely have enough time to do the things they should be doing, and finding 15 minutes of quality time per day per child is sometimes a futile dream. These parents are counting on the schools to take up the slack. The time bind that dual-career families experience on a daily basis translates into increased school stress for students, teachers, and administrators. Parents want educators who can handle all of their children's problems at school without bothering them at work, and latchkey kids and blended families also add stress to the equation.

Parents Who Are Fearful That Their Children Won't
Be Able to Measure Up Because the Schools Are Failing
to Provide Discipline, Basic Skills, and Values

Parents who see education as the answer to a better future for their children are concerned that watered-down curricula, lack of standards, and out-of-control student behavior will deprive their children of the skills they need to succeed in life.

Why Are So Many Parents Angry, Troubled, Afraid, or Just Plain Crazy?

There is an exercise I sometimes do in training sessions called "Walking a Mile in Another's Moccasins" (McEwan, 1997a, p. 152) that requires two opposing groups, who are not communicating effectively, to listen to one another and then paraphrase the opposing point of view. I used one half of the process with some parents before writing this book, asking them to tell me what kinds of experiences have made them angry, troubled, and frightened in their interactions with school personnel. Unfortunately, there were no educators present during the exercise to respond with their own points of view, but hopefully, you'll find the following list helpful as you try to understand and work with the parents in your school.

Parents Who Are Angry

The list of things that make parents angry is a long one, and although you may not be guilty of doing any of the things listed here, you will undoubtedly encounter parents who, based on their past experiences with other educators, will treat you as though you have. Before you get defensive and start making excuses, try to understand these parents. Be aware of the following reasons why parents are blowing their proverbial tops more frequently:

Failure to Communicate

This is the number one reason why parents get mad. Consider the principal who, 2 weeks into the school year, was authorized to hire another third-grade teacher to alleviate overcrowding. Jubilant at solving his problem, he never stopped to consider the importance of notifying the parents and students who were being reshuffled and displaced. Kids were upset, parents were furious, and the principal is still licking his wounds.

Making major changes without giving parents input or even notice has a way of making them seethe. Although public hearings, newsletters, advisory councils, and opinion polls do take a lot of time and energy and don't always give people what they want, the information sharing and discussion can defuse anger, quell rumors, and remove misconceptions. In a small eastern community, one solution to overcrowding was to move the kindergarten class to a vacant high school classroom. Imagine the rumors of children plowed down in the parking lot by power-crazed teens in hot rods. Consider the possibility of mere infants exposed to teens smoking and making out in the hallways. Or even worse, the prospect of drugs being offered to fresh-faced 5-year-olds. After public meetings and joint problem solving, an early childhood education program staffed by high school students (who received credit) proved to be an innovative educational offering that everyone could support.

But if lack of communication on the administrative level annoys many parents, failure to keep information flowing from teachers to parents makes all moms and dads mad. They hate surprises. In response to public outcry in one school district, a task force suggested mandatory midterm reports so that parents had to be notified of less than satisfactory grades (or behavior). Parents were tired of being blindsided at report card time by bad news. Consider this parent's experience:

> I feel so much frustration and anger when a teacher or administrator fails to communicate. This was the first sign of problems with Marcus's teacher last fall. There was no communication at all. Even when I went to talk with her so I could get a feel for how things were going, I learned very little.

Circling the Wagons

Automatically backing teachers against parents and kids without really hearing the issue from the parents' perspective or talking to the children involved ranks as number two on the list of things that make parents furious. I call this practice "circling the wagons." Many teachers feel that their administrator's first responsibility is to back them, no matter what they do. But when teachers are abusing children (psychologically or physically), wasting children's time, or freelancing with the curriculum, parents are hard pressed to understand why an administrator would defend or cover up for the wrongdoers.

Consider a case in Berkeley, California, where the school district is paying more than $1 million to settle a lawsuit brought by nine female students and five of their mothers that claimed the district failed to investigate sexual abuse complaints against a teacher. Because the teacher in question was a popular one, no one believed the students, and the wagons continued to circle even as the students were testifying against him in court (Walsh, 1996).

Stonewalling and Spinelessness

Saying you'll do something about a problem and then doing nothing or promising to call a parent back and then conveniently misplacing the message are other practices that makes parents climb the walls. Knowing that a disciplinary problem exists (e.g., bullying on the playground, smoking in the washrooms, rebellion in the lunchroom) or that a personnel issue is approaching an emergency (e.g., a teacher is harassing a student, instruction is ineffective, classroom is out of control) and choosing to ignore it out of fear, indifference, or just plain indecision is a risky business.

In a recent decision by a nine-member federal jury, a school district in Ashland, Wisconsin, was found guilty of discrimination against a gay high school student by failing to protect him from the verbal and physical brutality of his classmates. The case was settled out of court for nearly $1 million. This incident is a disturbing example of what can happen when pretending nothing is wrong becomes a way of life for administrators. Although the boy's parents repeatedly brought their complaints to school district officials, the abuse their son suffered at the hands of his classmates continued over a 6-year period ("A Lesson," 1996; "Gay Student Wins," 1996).

Damned If You Do and Damned If You Don't—Overreacting

Just when you think you understand the new rules about what can happen if you ignore problems, you abide by the letter of the law, and then everybody gets mad at you all over again. Mother said there would be days like this. But can you blame parents for wondering if educators have taken leave of their senses when they suspend a student for having Midol at school or for kissing a classmate on the cheek? By following the letter of the law in their overreaction to fears of being sued, some educators have become the brunt of talk show comedians and newspaper columnists (Riechmann, 1996, p. A4).

Assumptions and Stereotypes

Putting labels on parents because of their marital status, religious beliefs, sex, color, ethnicity, or socioeconomic status makes parents angry and justifiably so. Just because I go to church and want my children to learn phonics, don't label me as a right-wing Bible thumper. If I'm a single parent, don't assume that I neglect my children, and just because I'm poor, don't type me as a lazy good-for-nothing.

Defensiveness

Getting defensive whenever a parent questions our actions or motives is a natural, but unwise, reaction. Our behavior will surely escalate what could have been a calm discussion into an angry exchange on both sides. When we get defensive, we appear guilty, stupid, and dishonest. All of these postures only serve to inflame a parent who only wanted answers or explanations.

Breaking Promises

In the heat of the moment, educators sometimes make promises they can't keep. "The bus will stop right at your front door." The bus stop is a half a mile away. "Oh, yes, we'll be hiring a middle-school band director for next year." The school board decided to double up music teachers at its last meeting. "Even if we don't have a full class of students, we'll still have that fast-paced math class." There's only one student, and the class is canceled. Whether or not you're to blame for the change in plans (and you usually aren't), the angry parent will forever remember your broken promise and blame you.

Educational Jargon

Our inability as educators to explain what we're doing and why in language that parents can understand makes them mad. They suspect educators of trying to pull the wool over their eyes and not giving them credit for being intelligent. Linda Freeman, director of the Greater Cleveland Educational Development Center, believes that unless we do a better job of communicating in plain language, any efforts to bring about changes in teaching and learning will fail (Freeman, 1996).

Intimidation, Control, Power, and Blame

There are dozens of subtle ways we intimidate parents, most unintentional but nonetheless damaging. We send parents notices of meetings without bothering to check with them ahead of time about their availability. We don't tell them what the meetings are about. And once we get them into our offices, we sit behind large desks in oversized chairs and seat parents as far away from us as possible. Sometimes we're sarcastic, belligerent, or demeaning. We bring in armies of specialists and support personnel to overwhelm a lone parent, rather than asking ahead of time if there's someone he or she would like to bring along. We feel free to take telephone calls in the middle of a conference or leave parent meetings with no warning. We tell parents rather than ask them. We accuse them rather than listen to them. Here's what one frustrated parent had to say:

> I hate it when school officials say "You must do this for your child." I'm not a teacher. I have some skills, but teaching is not one of them, and it frustrates the hell out of me when the teacher tries to pin my child's learning failures on me, which, believe me, has frequently happened. After all, the teacher is the expert, right?

Condescension and Rudeness

Parents who are treated rudely and with condescension by educators carry the scars for a long time. They feel demeaned and powerless. Listen to the advice this parent (who recently had a serious mad-at-school experience) gives to administrators:

Treat parents as though they have brains in their heads (some of them might just be smarter than some of you). Don't ever be condescending in your response, and even when you know you're going to have to make an unpopular decision, practice diplomacy and at least hear out the opposition and validate their opinions.

Dishonesty

Principals don't tell outright lies very often, but when they do (usually to cover something stupid they did), the parent-principal relationship can be destroyed forever. Little white lies are seductive, but don't be tempted. "Hell hath no fury like a woman scorned," goes the oft-quoted phrase (Congreve, *The Mourning Bride*, act III, scene i). My paraphrase is "Hell hath no fury like a parent who's been duped."

Unwillingness to Admit Mistakes and Apologize

Every administrator has done his or her share of dumb things. Parents will usually forgive a mistake, bad judgment, or a momentary lapse of common sense. But what they can't abide is an unwillingness on the part of educators to admit the mistake and apologize. I collect "dumb" things that schools do, and in spite of all of the policies and supervision we have in place, they continue to happen. Fortunately, we're getting better at saying we're sorry. In Chicago, a computer teacher showed his 4th-grade class the R-rated movie *Striptease*. He violated school policy and used incredibly bad judgment, but the school district is admitting he did it and is recommending his dismissal ("Class Sees 'Striptease,'" 1997). Smart action on their part. In another case of "How dumb can you be?" a kindergarten teacher painted a child's face with an important message, believing that her prior handwritten messages to home were not being delivered. The superintendent apologized. No word on whether the teacher, who was suspended without pay, or her principal followed suit ("Teacher Pens Note on Face," 1996).

In the absence of common sense and an honest admission of wrongdoing, parents are increasingly turning to the courts to settle their grievances regarding problems that should have been handled at school. A Tucson, Arizona, parent filed a lawsuit after a teacher allegedly pulled her daughter by the hair while she was horsing around with a friend ("Lawsuits That Target Schools," 1996). The teacher denies doing anything wrong, and the student obviously wasn't an angel either. Perhaps the lawsuit is frivolous, but somewhere between the teacher's and the student's versions is truth, and apologies were obviously needed on both sides.

Failure to Give Parents Credit
for Understanding Their Children

Parents would like to have their personal knowledge and understanding of their children validated; they get angry when educators assume that the experts know best. One parent describes her frustration at being left out of the loop:

> One of the things that bugs me the most about school officials is that they think they know best, and personally, I think the parents usually know best. Officials get hung up sometimes on what they learned in school and start classifying kids. They are so sure a certain method will work with a child and don't bother to ask the parent's opinion.

Lack of Respect for Parents and Children

Administrators are frequently accused of treating parents who are educationally or economically disadvantaged without respect. And that makes the shortchanged parents mad. Administrators talk down to them or take advantage of them in ways they would never dream of doing with the PTA president or a CEO. Assigning the kids of so-called people-who-count to the best teachers, meting out discipline and awards based on parental pressure, or giving perks to a select inside power circle is very demoralizing to the have-nots. And don't think they aren't aware of exactly what's happening.

Being Asked for Advice and Not Having It Taken

Parents are often invited to be part of local decision-making groups, and they interpret these invitations as a genuine desire on the part of educators for their input. Too often, what educators really want is a rubber-stamp process that will allow them to say "we solicited parent input." Parents get angry and feel disenfranchised when the recommendations they make are rearranged or, worse yet, ignored.

Unprofessionalism

Administrators draw the ire of parents by doing things such as gossiping, sharing parental confidences, talking derogatorily in public about parents and kids, or looking the other way when teachers are guilty of these same practices.

Parents Who Are Troubled

As we have seen in the previous section, there are plenty of things that make parents feel negative and hostile. The emotional upheaval that occurs over an actual or perceived wrong stirs them up and makes them mad as hornets. Many will cool down after a day or two of reflection. But troubled parents are somewhat different. They experience a pervasive and long-standing worry. Their feelings of uneasiness, misgiving, apprehension, and disquiet fall into what I have labeled the "troubled" category. Defusing a parent's anger over a specific situation or instance, although often challenging, is a piece of cake compared to dealing with parents who are troubled. The concerns of these parents are more open-ended, less easily articulated, and yet more deeply felt. Their worries are connected to core values and may involve issues of politics, religion, and race. These feelings are more difficult to address because they often involve areas over which administrators have less control. Here are some reasons parents are troubled:

Lack of Student Learning, Schoolwide or Districtwide

Although many parents do not clearly understand the debate between phonics versus whole language or the difference between process writing and old-fashioned grammar and spelling, they are concerned about whether their children will learn to read and write. Being told to "trust us" by educators does nothing to assuage their worries. In fact, giving an answer like the following (Ledell & Arnsparger, 1993), to a question about whether implementing a new curriculum will improve student achievement, can be more disconcerting than reassuring to parents.

Not conclusively. . . . Right now, we don't have reliable ways to measure student's improvements in learning. Traditional standardized tests are inadequate measures of thinking skills, problem-solving abilities, creativity, communication skills, and teamwork. . . . The preliminary indicators of success mentioned earlier [higher graduation rates, better attendance, fewer discipline problems, more students going on to higher education, more comments about improved learning from students and parents], combined with the enthusiastic support of key educators, leading businesses, and many policymakers are sound reasons to have confidence that restructuring will increasingly be recognized as a successful approach to improving student achievement. (p. 20)

Lack of Learning or Behavior Problems Closer to Home

When a child is "falling through the cracks" and parents sense that no one is interested or able to respond, they get worried. One of the most frustrating situations for parents to handle is the average performance of a child who is very bright and is underachieving. Also included in the category of "child worries" are the following:

- My child isn't liked by school staff.
- My child is unfairly punished when other guilty parties are not.
- My child is bored and already knows everything that's being covered.
- My child is failing.
- My child is unhappy and socially unsuccessful in his peer group.
- My child is not given a chance to shine in sports, art, music, or other areas of personal achievement.

Erosion of Values

Many parents are also worried that what they hold dear in the areas of morality and decency is being ripped away from them. They watch in dismay as some schools hand out condoms (Berger, 1991), and a middle-school counselor tells parents it's none of their business when she takes their children to a county health clinic to receive birth control pills, Pap smears, and tests for the AIDS virus (Lindsay, 1996).

Pam Angelo, a parent in Antioch, California, objected repeatedly to a required 10th-grade course that asked students personal questions about depression, drugs, grief, and what their parents say at home. She didn't ask school officials to change the curriculum, only to have her children excused from the course. To accomplish her goal, she was forced to file a lawsuit. Only after winning the suit was her son allowed to enroll in an alternative class ("Lawsuits That Target Schools," 1996).

Parental Assault

There is a growing public perception that schools are undermining parental authority and co-opting parental rights (White, 1996). Dana Mack (1997) says, "At the heart of parents' frustration . . . is a deep unbridgeable chasm between the vocabulary of moral dictates, rules, and authority that parents think are best for children and the vocabulary of autonomy and 'choice' that emanates from the classroom" (p. 123).

Encountering curricula that encourage children to answer intrusive questions about their family life or to "reeducate" their parents about drugs, alcohol, and discipline has made many parents feel that an adolescent Gestapo is being trained; they are worried about it. Even if parents have not personally experienced any problems, their conversations with other parents and even teachers fuel the flames of controversy. Parents in Virginia recently flooded the Virginia Board of Education with calls to complain about a plan to increase the number of counselors in elementary schools, concerned that this move was just one more example of "social engineering" (Vest, 1997).

Curricular Issues

Nothing worries some parents more today than the curricula, library books, textbooks, programs, tests, and grades that their students are being given. And if you think that these concerns are coming only from individuals of a right-wing political or religious stripe, think again. Mary Damer (personal communication, July 13, 1997), founder of the Taxpayers for Academic Priorities in St. Charles Schools (TAPIS), Illinois, doesn't fit the mold. Involved since college in liberal politics, she met her husband, a history professor, at a peace march. Damer was worried enough about whole language, new mathematics, and low test scores (given the relative affluence of her community) to enroll her children in a Montessori school. "I kept waiting for a sense that things were improving in the public schools so I could send my children, but it hasn't happened yet." Now, she and a cohort of concerned parents are regularly publishing a newsletter that is asking some tough questions about accountability and responsibility. "The school district has been very hostile to us," Damer says. A former school administrator herself, Damer chuckled as she related the district's response to the questions she and her group initially raised about curricula. "They sent out packets to all of the teachers explaining how to deal with right-wing tactics. We just wanted to know whether there was any research to support the decisions they were making."

A school district in the middle-class Catholic community of Cranston, Rhode Island, tried to change the traditional ABC report card and got more than it bargained for when a group of "soccer moms" organized Parents for Quality Education to put a stop to their plans. Although the district had introduced a whole-language approach to literacy, process writing, and a revised math curriculum in line with the National Council of Teachers of Mathematics standards without encountering any resistance from parents, when they tried to revise their evaluation system to align with the curriculum, parents resisted big time (Olson, 1995).

Teacher Commitment

At the heart of many parental worries about schools is the teaching staff. Parents know that any given school year can be heaven or hell for their child depending on the teacher. Here is one parent's take on teacher commitment:

> I have a lot of respect for good teachers. My kids have had some really good ones, with whom I have worked well. They've also had some bad ones, who have been frustrating for me. Lazy teachers, inept teachers, rude teachers—they run the gamut. When my kids got really good teachers, I would do anything for them. Unfortunately, most of the good ones I've found are in

private schools. That's where people work because they love the kids, not money.

The perception that incompetent teachers are protected by unions and receive raises each year simply by staying alive rather than by producing results worries parents. Issues of competence, tenure, and the feeling of powerlessness that overwhelms them when their child has a bad teacher cause many parents to lose sleep.

Parents Who Are Afraid

In addition to being angry and troubled, parents are also afraid. Here are some of the things that scare them about today's schools:

Safety

A recent *U.S. News and World Report* article on school violence reported that more than 3 million crimes are committed in or near the 85,000 public schools of our country (Toch, 1993, p. 30).

To the dismay of some administrators in New Hampshire (who are probably embarrassed that they didn't do it first), a group of parents in Nashua, concerned about student bullying and intimidation, disorderly classes, and disrespectful students, has organized Citizens for Discipline in Schools. The parents say they were tired of waiting for stricter safety and discipline standards in their children's schools. They are lobbying throughout the state for the formation of other local chapters (Portner, 1996).

Administrator or Teacher Retaliation

Although I personally believe that actual retaliation against parents and children is infrequent, this fear is one that parents often mention when talking about school problems. They are afraid that if they complain about a teacher or a problem, their child will be the target of retaliation by the administrator or teacher or he or she will be perceived as a troublemaker and blacklisted forever. So they fret and stew in silence rather than tackling the problem head-on.

The Unknown

It's a brave new world out there, and the constant barrage of articles about the career challenges of the 21st century, the United States's lack of global competitiveness, and the need for students to have top-notch academic skills has parents running scared. They worry that their children won't be prepared, and they don't have time to wait for the research results. They want to know that we know what we're doing right now.

Having to Settle for Poor Schools

Financially secure parents can pay their bills and still choose the best public schools or the priciest private schools. But for families who feel they have no choice about their children's education, the fear of having to settle for second-rate schools is real. These parents look at test score rankings and school finance inequities and know immediately that their children are being cheated out of a quality education by virtue of where they live. Their fears are driving the voucher, charter schools, open enrollment, and school choice movements.

Parents Who Are Crazy

The final category of parents with whom you must deal is the "crazy" group. How can you identify such a parent? You know you've handled more than your share of them when (a) you're thinking about early retirement, (b) you have a year's supply of Maalox in your bottom desk drawer, and (c) you have the speed dial on your phone connected directly to the district's law firm. You cannot use rational methods with crazy parents. Oh, you will try, but be prepared for more than your share of failure and frustration.

School Groupies

These are parents on a power trip. Their life is centered in your school, and they won't go home. They want control, information, involvement, and more control. Their self-esteem is based on manipulating school personnel, and they are sick people. School groupies don't care about kids, even their own. In the beginning, they seem nice enough, but just don't cross them. They will harass you, trash you, manipulate you, and are perfectly capable of carrying out a personal vendetta against you that could ruin your career.

Abusive Parents

These parents are abusing their children either psychologically or physically. In cases that are documented, you are legally obligated to report the abuse to the proper authorities, but sometimes the abuse is less obvious and must be confronted in more discrete and subtle ways. Abusive parents don't feed their children, beat up on them physically and emotionally, seldom come to parent conferences, and can never be reached by phone.

Addicted, Dysfunctional, and Mentally Ill Parents

These parents consume mountains of time and energy as you attempt to help them and their children. They make promises they don't (or can't) keep, embarrass and humiliate their children, frustrate and clog up the system, lie, and frequently scare you to death with threats, harassment, and verbal abuse. Some are alcoholics, drug addicts, sexual perverts, and criminals. Many have serious mental illnesses. If you don't have any parents like this in your school, give thanks. But on the other hand, they may just be dressed up and in disguise.

Complainers, Troublemakers, and Whiners

These are parents with multiple axes to grind who like to attack people and not problems. They don't want anyone to do anything that might make things better for them or their children—it's just plain easier to complain. They don't like anyone, especially themselves. Their children can never please them either. And you, the educator, will come in for more than your fair share of abuse from these thoroughly disagreeable and unlikable people to whom you are expected to be gracious, warm, and accepting.

I hope you're not too depressed and demoralized after reading Chapter 1. The challenges in public education today are enormous, and the need for creative leadership and problem solving is critical. More parents than ever are angry, troubled, afraid, or even crazy. In the face of this onslaught, you must be calm, thoughtful, caring, intelligent, articulate, direct, and honest. In a nutshell, you've got to walk on water. If you feel unprepared to handle the challenges, don't be alarmed. You may need to develop a different repertoire of behaviors, strategies, and systems. Perhaps dealing with people who are upset comes naturally for you, but most of us need to work hard at keeping our own cool while we're defusing anger, informing the troubled, calming the fearful, and understanding the irrational. The chapters ahead will provide help for you by describing four important steps you can take to deal with difficult parents:

1. Defuse and disarm emotionally charged behavior.
2. Engage in productive problem solving.
3. Create a healthy school culture and climate.
4. Build parental support.

Chapter 2 includes dozens of strategies for defusing upset parents. Chapter 3 describes a generic problem-solving process you can use in almost any situation and addresses some of the most common school problems. Chapter 4 will help you analyze your school environment to discover whether you and your faculty may be unwittingly encouraging a dysfunctional "school family." Last, Chapter 5 will give you a proactive approach to building a supportive and involved parent community.

2

Strategies for Defusing Parents Who Are Angry, Troubled, Afraid, or Just Plain Crazy

> If you can keep your head when all about you
> Are losing theirs and blaming it on you;
> If you can trust yourself when all men doubt you,
> But make allowances for their doubting too:
> If you can wait and not be tired by waiting,
> Or, being lied about, don't deal in lies,
> Or being hated don't give way to hating,
> And yet don't look too good, nor talk too wise . . .
>
> —Rudyard Kipling (1936)

Learning how to defuse the negative emotions that parents who are angry, troubled, afraid, or just plain crazy bring into your office is a difficult but critical skill to master. In fact, your effectiveness as an administrator could well depend on your ability to "keep your head when all about you are losing theirs" (Kipling, 1936). Parents who are upset can throw temper tantrums, assault you verbally, or threaten to have you fired. Their feelings are obvious. But don't think for a minute that those parents who are more refined and polite are any less distressed. They've just learned how to package their feelings in more appropriate ways. Even though they arrive in Armani suits with polished presentations, their feelings are still the same. You can't afford to ignore either group of parents. Although their communication styles and approaches to problem solving may differ, the skills you'll need to deal with them (with a few exceptions) remain constant.

Why Do Parents Act the Way They Do?

In Chapter 1, we discussed dozens of reasons why parents might be upset with what's happening at school. And they do have reasons, whether real or imagined. There are two additional complicating factors: (a) Any problem or potential threat to someone's child will automatically bring out the worst in them, and (b) most parents have some personal and secret sensitivities that cause them to feel threatened, fearful, or uncomfortable in certain situations. Parents who have themselves known school failure, rejection, and prejudice will arrive at your school door with one set of feelings. Those parents who are accustomed to solving problems, having answers, taking charge, and getting their own way will arrive with a different set of expectations. Knowing the whys, wherefores, and backgrounds of each of the parents in your school family isn't possible (or even necessary), but understanding where a parent who is distressed is coming from can often turn confrontation into collaboration and keep a conflict from becoming a conflagration.

What Are the Best Ways to Handle Parents Who Are Worked Up and Worried?

Defusing distressed parents always requires a measure of on-the-spot situational decision making. However, the more systematic your approach to handling parental concerns can become, the more likely that you will feel confident no matter what or who comes walking through your door. There are numerous things you can routinely do that will help you deal effectively with parents who aren't happy. These same practices work well with anyone who's worked up or perturbed about something (e.g., teachers, students, children, spouses, or friends). Don't make the mistake of thinking, however, that because these behaviors are the obvious and common-sense things to do, they will be easy to master. Integrating them into your working life will take time and discipline. You will stumble and fail frequently. These are not behaviors most of us adopt naturally.

Rather, these simple suggestions require that you wrestle with your own personal values and beliefs and learn to manage your own emotions. Once you have these behaviors firmly established in your own repertoire, however, you will find problems solving themselves before your very eyes. The first two bits of advice that follow deal with trustworthiness and integrity, qualities of reputation and character that you must establish over time. They aren't "things to do" so much as "ways to be." With trustworthiness and integrity on your side, you will have "money in the bank" when it comes to dealing with unhappy parents. The remaining suggestions are more action oriented and advise you how to conduct yourself as you work with parents who are angry, troubled, afraid, or just plain crazy.

Ways to Be

Be trustworthy.

You can't make people trust you. They either do or they don't, based on your behavior, your reputation, or experiences they've had with someone in the same position as yours. Some parents may reserve judgment until they've seen you in action themselves, others will take the word of a friend or neighbor (the grapevine is alive and well), and still others will make up their minds about you immediately, based on nothing more than a gut feeling. Building trust among parents (as well as staff members and students) is one of the most important tasks you will undertake as an administrator. Trust is the glue that holds any relationship together through tough times. When parents trust you, they will give you the benefit of the doubt. They will approach you with an attitude of respect that says, "Even though I'm upset with you personally or have questions about the ways things are done here, I know that you're an intelligent, caring person who will try to understand where I'm coming from."

When you say or do something that violates the trust people have in you, the humiliation and embarrassment you feel is pervasive. I remember clearly and with total chagrin the day I lost the trust of one family in my school. I had spent years building the relationship, and I destroyed it in an instant with a carelessly spoken word. The family was a difficult one—three children with discipline, learning, and social problems. But we finally got everyone "on the same page" and were making progress. One day, after a particularly frustrating disciplinary encounter with the youngest child, I blew my top in the mail room adjacent to the office. My remarks, inappropriate and unprofessional, were overheard by mom, waiting in the hallway just outside the door. I apologized profusely, of course, but in just a moment of thoughtless venting, I had destroyed this family's faith in me as an advocate for their children and a trustworthy professional. I learned the hard way that day. Here are some other do's and don'ts:

- Never talk about people behind their backs. Don't ever verbally assassinate parents or children, even behind the closed doors of a confidential meeting. Your statements might still make their way back to the ears of parents.
- Don't make promises you can't keep.
- Do more than you promised you would.
- Apologize when you're wrong.
- Confront people with care and respect.
- Tell the truth in love.
- Do what you say you're going to do, and if you can't, let people know what's standing in the way of your following through.
- Build people up whenever you can.
- Be punctual.
- Be thorough and conscientious.
- Always attack the problem, never the person.

Have integrity.

Having integrity, the second important trait of character that gives you money in the problem-solving bank, consists of far more than just telling the truth. Integrity speaks of a unity and consistency of personal behavior that withstands the scrutiny and invites the confidence of parents. Educators of integrity are predictable because they make decisions out of a seamless and coherent set of values and beliefs. They know what they stand for and can articulate their beliefs with eloquence. If you make decisions and handle problems based on the three P's (politics, pressure, and power), you will soon have a reputation as someone who "blows in the wind," an educator who can be bullied and bought. With that kind of reputation, you can expect more than your fair share of parental problems. Consider your responses to the following questions as you begin to develop your own personal set of core values.

- What are the "truths that you hold to be self-evident"? (e.g., All children can learn and achieve. All of my teachers are capable and confident. Or, Teachers know best and parents shouldn't meddle in education. Kids today just don't measure up to our generation.) What you believe will dictate how you behave.
- What is the mission of your school?
- What are the nonnegotiables of your school (e.g., in the areas of discipline, respect, achievement)?
- What do you expect students to be able to know and do when they graduate from your school?
- What do you value most—people or procedures?
- How are decisions made—in a shared or solitary way?
- How is accountability determined (e.g., by how good you feel, how many new programs you implement, or how much students and teachers learn)?

Things to Do

In addition to having trustworthiness and integrity, there are many things you can do in your interactions with parents that can defuse anger and distress.

Shake hands and welcome parents into your office.

Even the most hostile parents will warm up to a personal greeting and a welcoming touch.

Sit eye to eye and knee to knee.

This simple statement is a key principle of group dynamics. It means that people need proximity to one another to engage in problem solving. When people are seated too far away from one another, the space between them inhibits communication. Don't sit behind your desk when meeting with parents. Sit side by side at a round table that could include other participants if needed. Provide comfortable chairs and offer coffee, water, or a soft drink (if available) to put parents at ease. Close the door so people can speak freely and make sure all phone calls and interruptions are held. These simple behaviors will send the message that you value and respect parents before a word is spoken.

Listen.

An important part of true listening is the discipline of *bracketing*, the temporary giving up or setting aside of one's own assumptions and prejudices to experience as far as possible the speaker's world from the inside (Peck, 1978, p. 73).

The very first thing to do when a parent with a problem comes to call is to listen. I personally have always had a very hard time listening. Impulsive and easily distracted, my mind has "a mind of its own." It could be wandering elsewhere, planning dinner, or making up a to-do list; I could be thinking of what I want to say in response; or I might be formulating the perfect solution to the problem being presented. I've learned the hard way that none of these approaches will win friends or influence people. Because I am also hearing impaired, I must overcome yet another set of challenges to effective listening. Men with mustaches and accents are my nemesis. If I lose the main idea, recovering it without looking stupid is difficult. I've also discovered that listening is a whole lot more than just hearing the words that someone is speaking. Their facial expressions, bodily movements, and tone of voice can communicate volumes about their true feelings.

It has taken me years of practice to perfect the art of what I call "wordless advice," not only with parents who are upset but with my own family members. I finally learned that when people come to me with a problem, they don't necessarily want my advice, they just want a sympathetic ear. They don't want my eyes to glaze over and my mind to drift to personal agendas; they want my full attention and thoughtful nods and "hmms." They don't want me to talk "at" them either. They need a sounding board, a place to reason out their own problems. By the time they finish their monologues, they thank me for the great advice (I never said a word) and go merrily on their ways. Here are some other tips to help you become a better listener.

- Notice the attitudes and feelings of individuals. They may communicate something different from what the words are saying. Posture, eye movements, hand gestures, tone of voice, and facial expressions are powerful communicators.

- Listen "between the lines" for what a parent is not saying in addition to what is being said.

- Do not respond with your own message by evaluating, sympathizing, giving your opinion, offering advice, analyzing, or questioning. Simply report back what you heard in the message as well as the attitudes and the feelings that were expressed.

- Keep your body language in harmony with openness, receptiveness, and attentiveness. Maintain eye contact, sit quietly without fidgeting, and arrange your hands and arms in a nonthreatening way. Don't frown, look alarmed, or make faces. Nod your head occasionally to indicate you understand the speaker.

- Make occasional and appropriate verbal responses, such as "Oh," "Hmm," or "Uh-huh," to confirm to the speaker that you are paying attention. Parents need to feel that you are understanding them both emotionally (e.g., their feelings of anger or fear) and intellectually (the actual words they are saying).

- Keep listening until there is a sign that the speaker has finished speaking and is ready to listen to you.

- Take notes about what the individual is telling you. Explain to the person that you are taking notes to help you remember critical details of the conversation. Most people with problems will be relieved to know that someone is finally listening to them and cares enough to write it down.

Open your mind.

Parents who are troubled and frightened often need permission and acceptance to share their private and very deeply felt concerns. If they sense that an educator isn't interested, doesn't care, or is passing premature judgment, they may well get cold feet and leave your office without having articulated the real problem. Parents need the freedom to explore an issue without criticism or censure. In the process, you may be exposed to a new point of view or an alternative way of viewing education, so suspend your initial prejudice or distaste and become a learner.

Keep calm; remain confident.

"To change a difficult person, you must first change yourself—your way of thinking about the person and your way of responding to the familiar provocations" (Tavris, 1978, p. 294). Most of us find it difficult to be neutral about parents who are angry and hostile. They bring out the worst in us. Maintaining your composure will effectively dismantle the hostile feedback loop that can be created if you respond in kind to angry words. As Tavris says,

> If you're pleasant and cordial, you will, in the long run, wear them down, even get them to be cordial back. It's surprising how often they warm up—not always, but often—because so often their hostility masks their own loneliness and insecurity. And in the long run, who benefits most by your being friendly and cordial? You do. (p. 299)

Your composure and courtesy will act as a mirror in which parents will find their own desperate attempts to intimidate and abuse embarrassingly and unattractively reflected. When parents sense your confidence, and they will, their bluster and bravado will diminish. If they sense fear and uncertainty, they will go for your jugular.

Establish time limits.

Establish a specific ending time for a meeting prior to its beginning, and you will find it easier to keep the discussion focused. If parents think they have an unlimited amount of time to state their case, they will take every bit of it.

Apologize.

Sometimes, the first words from your mouth, when a parent stops talking long enough to come up for air, should be an apology. In these litigious days, many educators are loathe to utter those words, fearing lawsuits and damages, but not saying you're sorry when you are obviously at fault will only exacerbate an already difficult situation. Accept blame. Often, if you're willing to take your share, parents will back down and admit they or their child might also be at fault. When my daughter was in high school, one of her favorite teachers called her a "bitch." Both she and I were understandably dismayed. I asked the principal to arrange a meeting for us with the teacher, the outcome of which I hoped would be a simple apology and an admission that a mistake had been made. That's all we wanted. If it had not been forthcoming, I can only imagine how much time and energy I might have expended on righting the wrong. But the teacher and the principal apologized. My daughter was able to ask the teacher for a college recommendation and everyone lived happily ever after. Except the teacher. He continued to make this same mistake over and over again. He was ultimately dismissed for sexual harassment, among other errors in judgment. But that's another story.

Get to the point.

See if you can get past the anger and frustration a parent brings to your office to the real issues and the bottom-line request. Often, this can be accomplished with a simple question when all of the grievances and concerns have been aired. "What do you want to see happen as a result of this conference?" If a parent cannot answer that question directly, then more discussion is needed.

Empathize.

Learn to lay aside your own needs to be heard and understood and focus instead on hearing and understanding what parents have to say. Perhaps, you have never had the identical experience they are having, but suspend belief for a moment and imagine yourself in their shoes. How would you feel? How would you act? Where would you go for help? Suppose your child were being evaluated for mental retardation. Would you be calm, trusting, and totally relaxed? I doubt it. Suppose your child were being bullied on the playground, and you thought no one cared. Would you take it lying down? Probably not. If you sincerely engage in this exercise of imagination, the parents with whom you are meeting will feel your empathy and begin to relax.

Ask questions.

Learn the power of asking the right questions to uncover all aspects of a problem. This process can be compared to the party gag of putting a small gift-wrapped box in increasingly larger and larger boxes, wrapping each one more elaborately than the last. Just when the person who is doing the unwrapping thinks he's about to get his "real" present, he discovers that the final box is empty. Sometimes in talking with parents, something similar will happen. Once all of the layers of confusion and misinformation have been peeled away, the problem may be nonexistent. Ask all of the usual "who, what, where, and why" questions. You may also find it helpful to use statements such as "I'm not sure I understand. Help me to see why this is so important to you." Offer alternative ways of thinking in the form of questions such as these: "Might it work this way?" or "What if we tried this approach?" When all else fails, ask for the parents' advice: "If you were in my place, what would you do?" or "Do you really think that would be a fair way of handling this problem?" Don't be afraid of asking open-ended questions to which you have no suitable answers. But beware of assuming the role of prosecuting attorney in your questioning mode. Clarification, not conviction, is your ultimate goal. There are a number of positive things that can happen as you question parents with whom you're meeting (Brinkman & Kirschner, 1994, p. 46):

- You will gather higher quality information than what is offered.

- You can help the other person become more rational.

- You can patiently and supportively demonstrate that you care about what they are saying.

- You can slow a situation down long enough to see where it's heading.

- You can surface hidden agendas and reveal misinformation without being adversarial.

Sometimes, strange and surprising things can happen if you are able to lay aside your own mental models (or paradigms) and consider alternatives. Mental models are "the images, assumptions, and stories that we carry in our minds of ourselves, other people, institutions, and every aspect of the world. Like a pane of glass framing and subtly distorting our vision, mental models determine what we see" (Senge, Keliner, Robert, Ross, & Smith, 1994, p. 235). Senge (1990) offers a variety of conversational recipes for turning encounters with people who are challenging or disagreeing with us into a discovery of their mental mode. For example, when faced with an impasse, Senge advises asking questions such as "Are we starting from two very different sets of assumptions here? Where do they come from?" or "It feels like we're getting into an impasse, and I'm afraid we might walk away without any better understanding. Have you got any ideas that will help us clarify our thinking?" (pp. 200-201). The notion that a conference with a distressed parent might actually turn out to be a learning experience for you as the administrator may be a somewhat revolutionary idea to consider, but drop your defenses and give it a try. Chris Argyris (1986, 1991), the noted organizational theorist, suggests that most skilled people in day-to-day communication must "unlearn" how to protect themselves from being threatened before they can ever become truly effective managers. If you are interested in learning more about how to do this, investigate a field of organizational development called *action science* (Argyris, 1990; Schein, 1992).

Speak gently and say the right thing.

The tone and quality of your voice are just as important as the words you speak. If you are hurried, hostile, defensive, or distracted, your voice will give you away immediately, and parents will judge you to be insincere, even if you're saying all the right things. There is an Old Testament proverb that says, "A soft answer turns away wrath, but a harsh word stirs up anger" (Proverbs 15:1, Revised Standard Version). A soft answer means that you don't contradict, correct, condescend, or disagree with parents who are already infuriated, even if they are obviously totally misinformed. Here are five other things (of many possibilities) to do when speaking to parents:

1. Meet parents on a personal level. Say something positive about their child. If possible, do your homework before the meeting. Look at the student's cumulative folder and consult with specialists (art, music, physical education, computer, learning center) to determine any special gifts or talents. One genuine compliment will help to set a positive tone for the conference.

2. Backtrack. This is a form of feedback in which you repeat back some of the same words or phrases that another person is using (Brinkman & Kirschner, 1994, p. 45). Although paraphrasing (dif-

ferent from backtracking) is often recommended as a way of confirming that you have understood what someone is saying, perceptive people often resent having their words replaced by your words. To them, that implies that you're twisting the meaning of what they've said. In backtracking, you don't echo everything that is said but instead, focus on key words that capture the main idea. This will let the other person know that you have heard and understood.

3. Give support and encouragement to parents who are distressed, by "be[ing] a clean mirror, [neither] descriptive . . . interpretive or judgmental" (Wegela, 1996, p. 160). Rather than judging or interpreting what parents are saying, hold up a mirror so they can see what their behavior may be doing to their children, to the teachers, or to themselves. Describe what you see, not how you feel about it.

4. At the close of the conference, summarize what you think you've heard. Not only is this a good-faith gesture that lets parents know you fully understand their point of view, but a brief review of critical information will clear up any misconceptions that may exist on either side of the table.

5. Conclude all conferences with a clear understanding of what was agreed on and what, if any, actions you or the parents will take. Ask parents if they are satisfied that their problem has been heard and understood. Even if the conference concludes without consensus, the knowledge that they have been heard and understood will defuse even the most anxious parents. Be sure to keep careful notes of the action items for immediate follow-up.

Redirect.

Often, parents who are perturbed want the principal or other administrator to do their "homework" for them. Let me explain. Suppose Mr. and Mrs. X are upset with Teacher Q. Rather than calling the teacher themselves to discuss the issue, they approach you and demand that the problem be solved for them. Your first question should always be, "Have you talked to the teacher about this?" If the answer is "No, we don't want the teacher to know we're complaining," then it's time to let the parents know that you'll be sharing exactly what they've said with the teacher anyway, and it would be far better for them to do it. If the answer to the question is "yes" and the parents can document several attempts on their part to solve the problem with no success, then it's appropriate for you to step in and facilitate communication between the teacher and parent or determine what is standing in the way of the problem being solved. But beware of being triangulated, (i.e., caught between two people who should be talking to each other but instead, have decided to put you in charge of their problems).

Lower the boom lightly.

There is an art to giving negative news, something you may well be called on to do in the course of meeting with parents who are upset. How do you tell a parent their child has no friends? How do you share the possibility that a child has a severe learning problem? How do you inform parents that their child is a thief and a liar? How do you communicate to parents who want to blame everything on you that they own a good share of the problem? Very carefully. With tact and gentleness. But with directness. Don't be so afraid of telling the truth that you never get to the point. Gauge how much information parents can comprehend at one time, particularly if the information is coming as a complete surprise to them. Don't babble and generalize. Speak simply and give concrete examples.

Welcome constructive criticism.

Perhaps the idea of welcoming constructive criticism from parents is as attractive to you as the prospects of oral surgery. But sometimes we need to hear and heed what parents have to say that might help us improve how we deliver education to their children. And even when the criticism is more destructive than constructive, we need to listen and to respond with openness, interest, and appreciation.

If you've made a mistake, admit to it. State briefly what you (or your staff, or both) have learned from the experience. Tell parents what you will do differently in the future to prevent the situation from happening again. Parents will respect you for your honesty and directness.

Don't react.

Reacting is acting without thinking. There are many possible ways to react that are inappropriate. Sometimes, our first inclination when cornered by an angry parent is to strike back (e.g., counterattack, defend, explain, justify, or just plain cut off and "divorce" parents you don't like). Instead, step back and remain neutral. Don't personalize the attack and try to convince the parent of their wrongness and your rightness. Equally ineffective is giving in just to get a parent out of your office and your hair, without regard for the child, any teachers who may be involved, or policies already in place to handle such situations. Be firm and stand your ground while solving problems. Having a reputation as a wimpy pushover is almost as bad as being labeled a terrible tyrant. Command respect. Neither run away from the problem nor gear up for battle.

Consider cultural differences in communication.

When the parents with whom you are meeting come from a different cultural background than you do, try to understand the subtleties that dictate their nonverbal behaviors and communication patterns. Nonverbal signals to consider include distance between people, eye contact, and whether touching is expected or appropriate. Who should initiate the conversation, whether interrupting is acceptable, and how to bring up difficult topics are also important considerations. If you are aware of cultural differences, you can alter your behavior patterns to put parents at ease and increase the likelihood of productive problem solving.

Take your time.

There is no rule that says every problem needs an immediate solution. Always take time to think; any decision (or upset parent) will benefit from a 24-hour cooling-off period. Never permit parents to back you into the "I've got to know what you're going to do now" corner. "The wise administrator knows how to create baffles and buffers to buy time, to absorb heat, to promote collective wisdom, to insure a maximum sense of legitimacy for final decisions" (Bailey, 1971, p. 225). Here are some ways to slow down the action:

- During the meeting, pause and say nothing, to give yourself time to gather your thoughts. During a long pause, you can sip your coffee or check your notes.

- Regroup by taking a few minutes to summarize the information or progress made thus far.

- Never commit to action that involves other individuals (especially teachers) without first consulting with them.

- Ask for time to gather more information or to consult with a superior. This sends the message that you are serious about solving the problem but want to make sure you're fully informed.

- If you feel your temper flaring and your blood pressure soaring, tell parents that you need to check on something with your secretary. Step out of your office, take several deep breaths, smile, count to 10, and return to your office with your composure restored. This is the administrative version of taking a time-out.

- When a meeting is headed nowhere (e.g., information is being repeated, tempers are beginning to flare, and nothing is being accomplished), perhaps it's time to schedule a follow-up meeting. Consider including some experts (e.g., a behavior management specialist to discuss some ways to improve time-on-task in the classroom, or the librarian to explain the book selection policy of the district) to help the situation.

Don't tell them; show them.

I remember well a conference with a second-grade student's parents. They were very angry that Michael had received a detention from the art teacher. Waving their copy of the form in my face, they demanded that I excuse Michael from serving it. "He didn't do it," they stated. Michael, as angelic as his heavenly namesake, smiled sweetly, fully expecting me to fall into line behind his parents. I invited the threesome into my office. The art teacher was not the type who overreacted. She must have had a good reason for her action. She had written a note at the bottom of the form explaining that Michael had hit the student who sat next to him. They gathered around my table—Michael, his mother, and father, all certain that I would see the "rightness" of their request.

"I'd like to hear about what happened in art class, Michael," I began. "Why don't you tell me about it."

Michael was suddenly having trouble remembering.

"Who sits next to you at your table?" I asked.

"Amy," he answered.

"Why don't we pretend that I'm Amy," I said. "And you can show me exactly what happened.

Reenacting the "crime" appealed to Michael's sense of the dramatic, and he immediately got into the spirit of things, showing me exactly how Amy's arm had rested on the corner of his drawing.

"Do you think she was doing that on purpose?" I asked.

"Nah," he replied, truthful at least in this instance.

"So, what did you do?" I asked.

"Well," he said, "I just touched her like this." He cocked his arm back and slammed his elbow full force into my ribs as his parents watched in dismay.

I caught my breath and said, "I see." And so did his parents. They probably wished for a hole to open up in the floor and swallow them up in their embarrassment. They'd been had by a 7-year-old. I was tempted to lecture them and nail Michael to the wall, but I resisted. I thanked them for following up and being concerned about Michael's progress.

"We appreciate your support. Don't ever hesitate to call us with a question or problem," I said. Sometimes, justice truly is served. This "picture" was worth a thousand words.

Don't fight 'em; join 'em.

When parents identify a problem in your school, enlist their help in solving it. When a group of parents came to see me about problems in the lunch room, I applauded their efforts, said we had already been discussing what could be done to make it a more appetizing experience for our students, and asked their help in creating a task force to study the problem. We all came out winners in that situation.

Give options to parents.

Don't back them into corners. Help them preserve their dignity. Allow them to save face. It's not about winning or losing; it's about solving problems for the benefit of children and their learning. Remember the goal.

Focus on problems, not personalities.

Stay focused on issues, and keep people and their flaws and faults out of the discussion as much as possible. When parents start tearing down people, redirect their attention to solving the problem.

Using these simple strategies, you'll be able to handle almost any parent who comes your way, and you'll do it with wisdom, understanding, and patience.

Things Not to Do

There are several responses you might make to parents who are upset that will backfire on you. Here's the short list of things not to do:

- Don't interrupt. Sit on your hands. Bite your tongue. Even if the person who's talking has made a mistake, don't jump in to correct it.
- Don't try to change the subject without giving notice that you're about to do so. Because my mind always seems to race off on my own personal tangents during conversations, I fight this no-no vigorously. When I do feel compelled to veer sharply from the agenda, I give the time-out signal from football and warn the person with whom I'm speaking. But to someone who's upset, changing the subject is highly inflammatory.
- Never focus on things that can't be changed. Concentrate on the alterable variables over which you, the parents, and the teacher do have control.
- Don't start complaining about your own agenda (e.g., attacking the superintendent or board of education for not giving you enough money to have the programs you want).
- Don't engage in silent combat (e.g., trying to stare the person down without saying a word).
- Don't start rehearsing your answer before you've actually heard and understood what the parent is trying to communicate.

- Don't advise unless you're asked.
- Don't try to persuade a parent that you are right and he or she is wrong.
- Don't try so hard to be neutral that you show no empathy.
- Don't come across as the know-it-all professional.
- Don't talk compulsively and overexplain, or you will raise questions in the minds of your listeners. "The lady [or principal] doth protest too much, methinks" (Shakespeare, *Hamlet*, act III, scene ii).
- Don't let yourself get backed into a corner by a parent who intimidates you. Think before you say "yes."
- Don't be so intent on smoothing a conflict that you achieve only a superficial resolution.

What Are the Best Ways to Handle Parents Who Fall Into That Rare but Worrisome Category of "Crazy"?

Parents who fall into this category require special handling. Just as you have challenging children enrolled in your school, you will also find challenging parents. And don't assume that the two necessarily go together. Two of the sweetest little boys I'd ever met were enrolled by a mother straight out of a B movie. She carried a .357 magnum (gun) on the front seat of her pickup truck and was never far from going over the edge. She scared me to death, and when my contact at the police department said she scared him too, I really got worried. The strategies that work with parents who are angry, troubled, or afraid may or may not work with parents who are also abusive, dysfunctional, dishonest, or just on a "power trip" at school. These parents require some special handling. Here are eight steps that can help:

1. Gather as much information as you can about the parent to help you understand behavior and motivations.

2. Keep careful and complete notes about all experiences and encounters with the parent. If you don't write it all down, sometimes you may doubt that it ever happened. But more important, the par-

ent may begin to lie or contradict, and you will need records of what was said and when. In some cases, you might even need a witness to confirm that a letter was sent or a document delivered to a parent.

3. Keep superiors informed. Mrs. Swanson was about to deliver her sixth child, and she had the three who weren't yet enrolled in school in tow when she exploded into my office with a problem. The techniques that usually worked with so-called normal parents were useless; she was out of control. "If you can't help me, I'll find somebody who will," she screamed, as she dragged her entourage of runny noses and unchanged diapers down the hall. I picked up the phone to let the superintendent know. It was a good thing. Five minutes later, the whole crew was sitting in his outer office refusing to budge until he gave them an audience. I was able to give my synopsis of the situation and explain what I'd done to try to solve the problem. Never underestimate the power of a "crazy" parent to wreak havoc. Get there first with the facts. Keep central office informed. They will appreciate your early warning system.

4. Consult with mental health professionals. If you are dealing with a parent who has a documented problem, learn more about it so you don't inadvertently say or do the wrong thing.

5. Consult with law enforcement officials. There have been occasions when I have asked for a police officer to be available in the school building during a conference with a potentially dangerous parent. You must protect your own safety and that of your staff members.

6. Know your school board policies, the legal rights of parents and students, as well as your own job description. There will be parents who have read all of these documents and be waiting to trap you.

7. Invite someone else to attend the parent conference to take notes or to witness what is happening. Use the special skills of the counselor, social worker, or school psychologist to help you defuse an explosive situation.

8. Be aware of the laws protecting the rights of children and your legal obligation to report any abuse of the children who attend your school.

How Can I Use My Encounters With Parents to Learn and Grow as a Professional?

Buddhists believe that we can and should be grateful for everyone who crosses our path. That point of view is a difficult one to embrace when we've just been raked over the coals by an irate parent. Why should we be grateful for someone who's out to make our life miserable? Or so it seems. But if you look on each encounter with a parent who's angry, troubled, afraid, or crazy as an opportunity to learn and grow as a person and professional, you will find yourself developing an entirely different attitude about dealing with challenging and difficult parents. Sometimes, in the midst of the harsh words and angry tempers, you will learn patience and forbearance. Often, while you're enduring frustration and embarrassment, you will reach deep within and discover a gift for helping others to solve seemingly insoluble problems. You will learn to channel your own feelings of anger and fear and in your strength, be a resource to parents who need wise counsel more than ever. As a result, their children will be more successful in school. Chapter 3 will describe the most common types of problem situations found in schools and suggest a model to help you solve problems productively.

3

The Most Common School Problems and How to Solve Them

> No problem is so large or complex that it can't be run away from.
>
> —Charlie Brown
>
> The mere formulation of a problem is often far more essential than its solution.
>
> —Albert Einstein

Defusing and disarming the emotionally charged parents who arrive on your doorstep is only the first step. Then, you have to help to solve the problem(s) that created their anger, fear, and distress in the first place. I do hope you love problems if you've chosen a career in educational administration. I personally love a challenge. I even get bored when there aren't enough of them, so I write a weekly question-and-answer column for parents and guest on several parent call-in programs. Of course, solving problems on the pages of a newspaper in 600 words or giving a 30-second answer on the radio is nothing like solving problems with real-life people.

If you don't love problems, even enough to go out looking for them, you're probably miserable in a leadership role. If your teachers and parents ever get the feeling that you don't want to hear bad news, you won't. Everyone but you will know "the sky is falling." There are many ways you can avoid uncovering and facing problems:

- Make it clear that anyone (parent, student, or teacher) who brings you a problem is rocking the boat.
- Avoid asking open-ended questions of parents, students, and teachers, such as "How are things going?" or "Are you feeling good about school this year?"
- Get bogged down in administrivia so you will be too busy to handle any problems (this will leave your secretary and others to pick up the pieces).
- Keep your schedule so tightly structured that it will protect you from the real world, which is teeming with problems of every kind.

What Kinds of Problems Are Out There?

School problems come in all shapes and sizes. They occur in the classroom, on the playground, in the lunchroom, and on the bus. Sometimes, kids notice them first, or sometimes, parents call us with a concern. But more often than not, educators identify the problems at school and then have to decide how best to resolve them. School problems that are ignored or left unsolved can result in unhappy parents, and when parents are upset, chances are their children will be doing less than their best in school.

For purposes of our discussion, a *school problem* is defined as anything that keeps a child from achieving his or her learning potential. Sometimes, school problems can be solved with a simple telephone call or a brief parent-teacher conference. Sometimes, a long-term, comprehensive intervention plan is needed. But if ignored, a real school problem can grow like an out-of-control weed, choking communication between home and school, cutting off trust and cooperation, and stifling the academic growth of the student. Let's look at the three major sources of school problems in more detail.

Problems Identified
by School Personnel

Educators specialize in identifying problems, although I've often felt like we're much better at finding them than at solving them. Skilled teachers can often identify several children with problems before the first week of school is over. The best teachers give children some time to settle in, do what they can to solve a problem at school, and then notify parents that all is not well.

The concern may come in the form of a telephone call, a handwritten note, or a formal report card. The phrases are usually polite and couched in educational jargon, but the meaning is quite clear to parents: "Your child isn't measuring up to some standard of behavior or achievement and you as a parent need to do something about it."

"Mary seems a bit immature with regard to her social relationships."

"I'm concerned about John's behavior. He isn't following our classroom rules, and none of my usual strategies seem to be working."

"Sarah is falling behind in her work. She has failed the last two math tests, and if she doesn't spend more time studying for the next quiz, she might receive a failing grade."

"Your daughter can't seem to get along with anyone. She wants her own way no matter what the situation."

"We're concerned about a possible learning problem with your son, Jeremy. Could you call and make an appointment for a conference at your earliest convenience?"

"Jessica doesn't seem quite ready for first grade. She hasn't learned her letter sounds and often has a difficult time paying attention when we read stories in the circle."

"Ken hasn't turned in his science homework for over a week. Can you give me a call right away?"

It took me awhile to realize that the majority of parents have done the very best they know how. It's not as if they purposely raised a child who can't or won't learn or tried to bring up a child to break all the rules in the book. So when they're faced with the prospect of their child's problems in school, their stomachs tighten into knots, they relive their own failures as a student, and immediately they launch into a cycle of self-blame and recrimination or adopt a defensive position that lays the blame squarely on someone else. For parents, finding solutions to the problems with which educators confront them usually involves facing difficult choices about themselves and their children, often requires large investments of time (and money) on the part of everyone involved, and may mean substantial changes in attitudes and behaviors. Tough choices. Hard work.

A problem of this nature faced Joan and her middle-school daughter, Tammy. Tammy had always been a bit of a social butterfly, preferring to talk with her friends instead of paying attention in class. Everyone thought she was bright but just not motivated. Her teachers found new and creative ways to describe Tammy on her marginal report cards, but the bottom line was always the same. Tammy just didn't work hard enough. Her bouts with depression and low self-esteem as she entered middle school sent Tammy and her parents to a veritable army of doctors looking for the underlying cause of her problems. Extensive neurological tests and subsequent counseling revealed a seizure disorder and a severe case of attention deficit hyperactivity disorder without hyperactivity. Joan is now working closely with school personnel but had to overcome some feelings of anger about the years of blame school personnel had laid on both her and Tammy.

Academic, social, or behavioral problems at school can frequently be manifestations of family problems as well. I recently received some rare positive news from a family who had once attended my school. I'll never forget the year I tried to help Sandra, the fourth grader, find some success. Everyone owned a share of this particular schooling problem. Sandra was uncooperative and sullen. Her teacher was punitive and rigid. Sandra's mother was hysterical. Only Sandra's father, who had deserted the family before she was born, was uninvolved. I attempted to move this trio through some problem-solving exercises but felt like a miserable failure. Sandra barely scraped through fourth grade, but I hung in with her family. As the years unfolded and I heard news of Sandra's teenage pregnancy and running away from home, her problems with homework and assignment completion in fourth grade seemed minor. But I also learned of the sexual abuse, alcoholism, and other dysfunctional behaviors that were a part of the home setting. They had all taken their toll on Sandra's ability to succeed in school. News of a solid remarriage for Sandra's mom, counseling and rehabilitation for Sandra, and her subsequent return to the family gave the Christmas greeting a happy note, but these changes had taken 8 years of heartache and suffering to achieve. The message in Sandra's story is that some schooling problems can often be symptomatic of a variety of family problems and cannot be truly solved until the family problems are tackled.

Problems Identified by Parents

Sometimes, parents identify school problems on their own. The problem may revolve around a poorly constructed curriculum, books and materials they find unacceptable, poor classroom management on the part of their child's teacher, or lack of achievement expectations in their child's classroom or school. School problems that affect the overall positive attitudes of parents about the school (or school system) can often have a very detrimental effect on their children's abilities to be successful and well-adjusted in the school setting. These problems are often systemic in nature and frequently take major change to remedy.

In some cases, parents are unwilling to wait for change and select another schooling option. A vivid example of just such a schooling problem played itself out in the newspapers, school board meetings, and local elections of my community a number of years ago. A group of parents vigorously objected to the use of a textbook series in the district's classrooms. This schooling problem did not come from the students, the majority of whom seemed largely unaffected by the curriculum until their parents raised concerns. And the teachers and administrators obviously didn't think the materials were a problem; they had chosen them. But judging from the emotional fervor, parents were most definitely concerned about the detrimental effects of the books on their children. After a task force reviewed the materials and recommended they be retained and the candidates who wanted to remove the materials from the classrooms were defeated in the election, a group of parents filed a law suit asking that their children be allowed to select an alternate curriculum of study and won. But the anger and distrust had left its mark, and many parents withdrew their children. Administrators were left to deal with the fallout.

Problems Identified by Students

The final category of school problems are those identified by the students themselves. If parents are regularly talking with their children and listening to what they say, there are often clues regarding potential problems in their comments.

"The teacher doesn't like me."

"I don't understand a thing that's going on in that class."

"I got a D on my last math test."

"Nobody likes me."

"My lunch was stolen out of my locker."

"I got put back in a lower reading group today."

"I'm in the dumb class."

"I don't understand my homework."

All children complain about school occasionally. Learning to distinguish between a real problem and the everyday ups and downs of life in a school is a critical skill for administrators (and parents). Every school day will not run smoothly for every child, and part of growing up is learning to deal with our imperfect world. But when the complaints are constant and revolve around a central theme, or when they begin to affect appetite, sleep habits, or personality, that's a warning that a serious school problem is in the making (McEwan, 1992). Don't try to pass off complaints as unimportant or a figment of a child's imagination. My experiences as a parent, teacher, and administrator have shown me that children are sensitive human beings with important perceptions about their schooling experiences. If for any reason they aren't happy in school, we need to do all we can to get to the bottom of their anxieties. Any problem faced by a child at school is a real problem that must be addressed. Sometimes, all we need to do is listen and empathize. But often, action is needed.

One of the regular ways I attempted to take the "pulse" of my school as an elementary principal was to eat lunch with small groups of students. In these informal settings, I would often uncover potential problems as students honestly shared their feelings about what was happening in their lives. I attempted to do the same with my own children as we talked about their daily lives at school around the dinner table. The challenge lies in sorting out what is a real problem that needs action and what is a minor problem that will solve itself given the passage of time. In many cases, children know before the rest of us that they have a problem. They just can't always explain it in ways that parents and teachers can really understand. After spending time listening to hundreds of students' and parents' cries for help, I responded by writing a series of books for parents, the titles of which are taken from quotes of students I have known: "Nobody likes me," "The dog ate it," "I hate school," and "I didn't do it" (McEwan, 1996a, 1996b, 1996c, 1996d,).

What Are the Characteristics
of Good Problem Solvers?

The characteristics of good problem solvers are amazingly similar to the qualities one needs to be a good parent or marriage partner: patience, discipline, creativity, continuous improvement, repetition, honesty, and continuous learning (Lynch & Werner, 1992, p. 160). Problem solving is always a part of quality decision making, but solutions do not come without struggle, frustration, and occasional bouts of chaos and messiness from time to time.

What Are the Seven Steps
to Effective Problem Solving?

Every theorist has developed his or her own model of problem solving, but most include some variation of these seven steps as "must-dos":

1. Gather all the facts and define the problem. Rushing to judgment or stating your opinion about a situation before you have listened to the various sides will often result in solving the wrong problem. Very few educational problems need immediate solutions, and the more information you have at your fingertips, the more likely that a quality solution will present itself. Some possible sources of information include observations, test scores, historical data, and consultations with a variety of specialists. Find someone on your student support team whom you trust and use that individual as a sounding board for thinking out loud.

2. Identify some possible reasons for or sources of the problem. Beware of responding too quickly with your own expertise. You may know exactly what is needed, but even if you are absolutely correct in your assessment, the other parties involved in the problem (e.g., teacher, parent, student) will need time to reach the same conclusion. I've worked with parents who needed several months to recognize what was best for their child, and if we had not given them that time and space, we would have frustrated our ultimate goal of helping the child.

3. Verify the most likely causes. Sometimes, finding a cause is impossible and a waste of everyone's time. In other situations, determining the cause is a guarantee of a quick solution.

4. Identify several possible solutions. Rare is the problem that has only one solution (even in math), so don't get committed to your solution too early in the discussion. You will shut down the creativity of others and may miss the best one. On the way to determining a solution to the problem, avoid blaming the child, the parents, or the teacher. Assigning blame is counterproductive and anger evoking. Assume that everyone has done the best they know how up to this point. If behavioral changes (in parent, teacher, student) are called for, someone (with administrative know-how and leadership) will have to provide help for the needy parties (e.g., staff development, behavior management support, parent training, counseling, etc.) Just telling people to change will not work.

5. Determine the solution that seems best, and then develop an action plan to implement it. An important part of developing the action plan is to make sure that all of the participants know the why, who, what, where, and when of the plan. I have seen many wonderful plans fail for lack of accountability. Everyone should know why the plan has been designed (e.g., to improve homework completion, to raise reading achievement, or to improve a student's time on task). All of the participants (who) should know the exact actions (what) they're supposed to take. Put the behavioral expectations in writing, and make sure everyone has a copy, including the child. Include a time line in the plan (when), and also include the location (where) in which the activities will occur. Anything that is left to chance will not happen.

6. Implement the plan. Make sure you give the plan enough time to work.

7. Evaluate and fine-tune the plan. Look for concrete evidence of success (e.g., more assignments turned in, fewer unacceptable behaviors, more positive interactions between parent and teacher, etc.).

Be forewarned that as you move through the problem-solving process, there are three possible scenarios that can occur.

Three Problem-Solving Scenarios

Consensus

If consensus is reached, all the players (parent, teacher, principal, child) agree on the nature of the problem and the solution. There could be some minor differences but not enough to hinder solving the problem. Parents are supportive of school personnel's plans, and they are going to do everything they can at home to help. Sharon's case is a perfect example of consensus and collaboration. Everyone agreed that Sharon had a serious problem. She was in third grade and didn't know how to read. She had transferred in from a private school where her learning problems had fallen through the cracks due to constant turnover in teaching personnel during her first-grade year. We tested Sharon, and it was clear that she had a learning disability. We immediately gave her special services and prescribed activities for her parents to do at home. We also talked with Sharon about what her part would be. Everyone followed through and did their part, and by sixth grade, Sharon was reading above grade level and winning awards in reading. Not every problem has such a successful resolution, but it is an example of what can happen when everyone, including the child, cooperates.

Compromise

Sometimes, there is disagreement as to the nature of the problem or the type of solution that is needed. In that case, a compromise may be reached. Both parents and school personnel agree to disagree on one or more issues but do so in the spirit of cooperation and together are able to work for what is best for the child. Compromise was the result of a problem-solving conference held with Mr. and Mrs. Stafford and their sixth-grade daughter, Joanna. Joanna had a serious personality conflict with a newly assigned teacher (hired to replace a teacher on maternity leave), and the situation had gone from bad to worse. The new teacher felt that Joanna was an indulged and spoiled adolescent. Her parents felt the new teacher was incompetent. Joanna was driving a wedge between the school and her parents. The principal was caught in the middle. The Staffords wanted an immediate change in her placement but agreed to a temporary plan designed by the teacher, the principal, and Joanna. There wasn't complete support from home, but the Staffords agreed to wait and see before pressing the transfer issue any further. We managed to make it to the end of the school year without bloodshed.

Confrontation-Capitulation

When there is no agreement and little promise for consensus or even compromise, the result is confrontation or capitulation or both. If a parent wants a course of action to be taken that school personnel do not find acceptable, or school personnel want a course of action to be taken that parents cannot support, an impasse is the result. Effective administrators and teachers always keep looking for ways to solve problems, but if an administrator is unwilling to negotiate or a parent is intractable, capitulation is the only answer. Although this is clearly a last resort, finding another schooling option for a child may be the only solution. Remember, however, that the goal of problem solving is to find a way to help each child be successful in the academic, behavioral, and social arenas.

When Should Parents Consider Another Schooling Option?

I have counseled many parents who are ready to select another schooling option when they feel that a problem is not being addressed to their satisfaction. Here's the advice I give them, and you may find it helpful as a basis for discussion with the parents in your school.

When to Stay

Counsel parents to stay where they are when everyone agrees on the problem and is willing to work on a solution. As wise as parents often think they are, they sometimes don't know a good thing. Help them to see that rushing off into an unknown situation before giving all the players a chance to work on a solution to the problem is a mistake. Encourage parents to give a "problem" teacher a chance to make some changes in the classroom. Try to show them the benefits for both child and teacher of working through an issue.

Advise parents to stay where they are when they are fully cognizant that the problem is their child's and that he or she has the ability to do something about it. If the problem is the child's problem and only his or hers, then moving to a new setting will not solve it. Moving will only confirm for the child that if he or she doesn't want to shape up or conform, all he or she has to do is complain and Super Mom and Dad will come to the rescue. Sometimes, children do need a fresh start, but give them every opportunity to solve the problem where it started. They will feel better about themselves if they can.

Suggest that parents stay where they are if the school year is almost over. Everyone gets tired after nearly 9 months of hard work. Encourage parents to talk about the decision over the summer when life is less pressured. The decision doesn't need to be made overnight.

Explain to parents the benefits of staying where they are if it appears that their child is manipulating the situation to get what he or she wants without a sincere desire to change. Some children are masters of manipulation. They know that if they can convince their parents that the problem belongs to someone else, they won't have to "face the music." This may be a hard sell for the parent whose child can do no wrong, but be direct and honest (but kind) in your assessment of the situation.

If parents are in the middle of a family crisis, caution them about the wisdom of making a change. Making a decision about schooling for a child when a family is in crisis is a big mistake. There might not even be a schooling crisis once the family problem is resolved. Help them to determine if schooling is really the problem or if some other problem is masquerading as a schooling problem. Often, a family counselor can help parents see the situation more clearly.

When to Leave

There are some good reasons for parents to consider transferring out of a school situation. It is hoped that you will be able to solve the problems they face before that has to happen, but sometimes, solving the problem will take longer than parents are willing to wait. Here's what I advise:

Parents should consider transfer when their child is constantly harassed, bullied, or is in danger. The problem of playground bullies exists everywhere, but if teachers and administrators are powerless to deal with them, it's time to transfer. Parents (and teachers) should teach children strategies for dealing with bullies, but without effective adult support, life will be miserable for a victim. Children who have different values or who are sensitive or gifted can often be singled out for verbal, if not physical, abuse.

Parents might be wise to transfer a child if he or she has become involved with the wrong peer group. A child's friends become more important to him or her with each passing year of school, and if a child has friends who are influencing him or her to act in unacceptable ways, then parents need to take action. Parents need to be reasonable in their judgments, but if they can document a decline in their child's motivation, attitudes, respect for family rules, and moral standards, that is genuine cause for alarm.

If a child is regularly being exposed to drugs, sex, and violence, a transfer is mandatory. If children have to worry about drugs, sex, and violence as part of their daily environment, they will have little time to concentrate on learning. And neither will anyone else.

Parents should definitely consider a transfer when a child is failing with no hope of rescue. No child should fail in school. There's no reason for it. Perhaps, with a fresh start in a new setting, a child can begin anew.

When parents object to everything that is done, you can politely recommend that they consider another schooling option for their child. There are some parents who major in criticizing everything that happens in a school. They lie in wait, ready to pounce on a library book with a bad word, a teacher who took a misstep, or a policy that is inconsistent. Their children will be much happier if they don't constantly have to worry about how every little thing that happens to them in school is going to affect their parents.

Sometimes, there are unfortunate personality conflicts, and people have said all the wrong things at the wrong times. *Reconciliation* and *conflict resolution* are wonderful buzz words, but when an unresolvable conflict between school personnel and parents exists, kids suffer, and parents seriously need to consider leaving. Children know when the people who are important in their lives aren't getting along. They suffer when their parents disagree over things, and they also suffer when their parents and teachers don't agree. Parents must be able to support the schools wholeheartedly.

I recommend to parents that they transfer when the teachers are poor, and no one will do anything about it. There are poor teachers everywhere. Some of them are very nice people; they just can't teach. Some of them aren't even very nice. If a child gets one of those people and there's nothing the parents can do to get their child into another classroom, they should look for another school. Nothing should stand in the way of their child's learning. There's too much to accomplish to waste a year in an unproductive situation. A child will spend more than a thousand hours in a self-contained elementary classroom during one school year. That's a lot of time to spend with someone who isn't top-notch. Remediating or releasing ineffective teachers takes time, documentation, and due process. In the meantime, some poor class of kids is going to pay the price. I've been there—in both my personal and my professional lives.

In the opening chapters of the book, we've focused on how educators can deal with parents who are angry, troubled, afraid, or just plain crazy: (a) We can help to defuse their emotions and (b) we can facilitate solutions to their problems. But there are also proactive steps we can take to reduce or eliminate out-of-control emotions and problem situations: (a) Create a healthy school climate characterized by accountability and communication, and (b) make parents a part of your school team.

4

Promoting a Healthy School: How to Tell If Your School Is Sick and How to Make It Well*

> There is a subtle spirit that exists in a school, both in the minds of the teachers and students and in every act, which may never be exactly described or analyzed, but which even the most inexperienced observer recognizes when he enters a school or a classroom.
>
> —L. J. Chamberlin (as quoted in Lindelow & Mazzarella, 1983, p. 169)

We usually talk about health in terms of our bodily systems, but organizations and institutions can also be described as healthy or unhealthy. Just as in a healthy body, all of the parts work together to achieve balance, in a healthy organization, there is also a sense of wholeness and soundness. A healthy organization provides an environment in which all the players have the capacity to respond to the challenges that bombard the system every day in order that its integrity and wholeness can be maintained. Just as our human body is constantly under attack by a variety of bacteria and viruses, there are "diseases" that can momentarily or even permanently disrupt the internal balance and health of a school. Don't be confused by thinking that a healthy organism (whether a human being or a school) is one that never comes under attack. Even the healthiest of living things are subject to a constant barrage of disease-producing

NOTE: Excerpts from *Healthy Congregations: A Systems Approach* by Peter Steinke are reprinted with permission from The Alban Institute, Inc., 7315 Wisconsin Ave., Suite 1250W, Bethesda, Maryland 20814-3211. Copyright 1996. All rights reserved.

microorganisms. But the healthy human or organization is able to respond to disease with antioxidants, immune systems, and healing powers. Just as the presence of disease signals our body to begin the healing process (e.g., a higher body temperature to kill germs), the awareness of disruption, distrust, anger, or frustration in an organization should cause its members to immediately mount an offensive against the unwelcome intruders. Knowing just what germs and diseases are most prevalent can help you diagnose and remediate your potentially ailing school. These infectious invaders can come both from without (the virulent viruses that parents carry into your school) and within (the culture and climate that you and your faculty have created together).

What Are the "Virulent Viruses" That Parents Can Carry Into Your School?

The viral infections that angry, troubled, frightened, or just plain crazy parents can bring into your school are much like the viruses that invade the human body. The healthy human body abounds with viruses (much like your school will always have upset parents). For a virus to do any harm in your body, however, it needs to interact with the body's healthy cells. It does this in very clever ways, tricking the host cells into thinking it's something that it's not. The host cell then innocently provides the virus cell with nourishment and a warm place to live, and the virus begins to grow and multiply. A virus has several interesting characteristics that are also found in many out-of-control parents (Steinke, 1996, p. 56):

- It cannot say "no" to itself.
- It has no boundary, respects no boundary.
- It cannot regulate itself, goes where it doesn't belong.
- It has no ability to learn from its experience.
- It cannot sacrifice for the sake of other cells.
- It is an intracellular parasite with no life of its own.

For out-of-control parents to do any serious damage in your school, they need to find "host cells," individuals who reinforce and even applaud their behavior (e.g., other parents, teachers, and even you, the principal). In the absence of strong leadership to confront these individuals and hold them accountable for their inappropriate behavior, parental viruses can be fatal. In and of themselves, however, they pose little threat. Here are the potentially serious six:

1. Clandestine Operations

There's never anything to worry about when everything is being done out in the open, but when people go underground, trouble begins. Secrets, closed meetings, whispering, and gossiping are the hallmarks of this virus. Healthy schools are open environments where honesty and integrity prevail. Individuals who thrive in secrecy are insecure, dependent, and childish. Their hidden agendas, insincerity, hypocrisy, and deception are behaviors that need to be confronted and eliminated. Strong leadership by both administration and staff is needed.

Here's an example: Ruth Rushton, the Parent-Teacher Association (PTA) president, had mounted a smear campaign against the new principal who refused to bow to her power grab. Ruth's tactics were typical of those who thrive on accusations: gossip, a petition drive, and secret meetings. Bringing her campaign out in the open was difficult but not impossible. The principal responded by inviting Rushton, key communicators, and parent leaders to an open forum where she confronted the lies with equanimity and confidence.

The principal refused to accommodate Ruth's unhealthy fusion with the school and her behind-the-scenes machinations; she exposed them in face-to-face meetings, and once again the school regained its healthy status. Remaining silent in the face of clandestine operations is unhealthy.

2. Faultfinding and Blame

Parents who are unwilling to take the responsibility for helping to solve problems turn instead to blaming everyone else. "You haven't taught my child." "If you were doing a better job, my child would have more friends." No matter what the problem, we are supposed to fix it. The "blame virus" needs a host cell to grow, and it will find one in the person of a principal who spends all of his or her time reinforcing the accusations by defending, explaining, justifying, or trying to "fix" it. The healthy leader will be able to recognize the faultfinding virus for what it is and realize that these accusations do not define him or her or the school but rather, define the individual doing the accusing. Carriers of the faultfinding virus are easy to identify. Faultfinders will never be happy, even when the problem is solved. Mrs. Michaelson was a big-time carrier of the faultfinding virus. We were to blame for everything, even her health. If her son weren't having so many problems in school, she wouldn't have high blood pressure. We listened but refused to take ownership of her problems, continually holding both her and her son accountable for their behavior.

3. Backyard Gossip

Parents who spread every rumor and half-truth blowing in the wind can often contribute to an epidemic of misinformation. Backyard gossip may seem harmless enough in the beginning, but if you have a critical mass of parents in your school who do not seek out the source when there is a problem but instead take it to their backyard bull sessions, you've got a problem. One of the most important ways to check backyard gossip is by providing everyone with adequate information. As surely as people do not have information, they will make it up. Their alternative to having the truth is to invent something and then react to their invention.

4. Lies, Half-Truths, and Slander

Parents with this virus often appear to be "righteous," but they are subtle in their manipulative and deceptive behavior. They are dangerous and downright wicked. I believe they are the most difficult parents to handle because their frames of reference are so impossibly different from ours that we fail to recognize them for what they are—liars. Scott Peck's (1983) book, *The People of the Lie*, offers remarkable insights into this virus. If you are dealing with a liar, you'll need all the help you can get.

5. Triangulation

The fifth virus is an easy one to overcome once you recognize its symptoms. Triangulation is when you find yourself in the middle of two people who should be talking to each other, but almost without becoming aware, you have taken on the role of go-between. Here's how it works. Mrs. Smith comes to you because of a problem her son is having in fourth grade. The teacher doesn't treat her child fairly. She wants you to solve the problem with the teacher (of course, without telling the teacher of her conversation with you). When you ask Mrs. Smith if she's talked to the teacher, of course the answer is no. There is a Swahili proverb that says, "When elephants fight, it's the grass that gets crushed." Guess who's playing the part of the grass in the class play this week! Parents will always try to triangulate because it's the easiest thing to do. If they can shift their anxiety to you, they'll feel terrific and the problem will become yours. Don't let it happen. Always send people to the sources of their anxiety to solve their own problems. Or, as a last resort, offer to facilitate a meeting where both parties are present. Now, when the source of a parent's anxiety is the child, a personal problem or mood they have, or a spouse, no one at school will be able to solve the problem. There is absolutely nothing to do but set definite boundaries and recognize who really owns the problem. Clearly, it is not the teacher's, the principal's, or the school's problem. However, that won't stop the parent from trying to triangulate!

6. The Friendly Enemy

The sixth and final virus can put you flat on your back before you realize you've even been exposed. Saboteurs do not wear signs announcing they are out to undermine your leadership or destroy your credibility. They are most often gracious, supportive, and generous with compliments (at least to your face). But their compliments always leave you feeling slightly less than self-confident and wondering just what was intended. As soon as you gain power or popularity, the friendly enemy will begin working to erode your support. These parents don't like the idea of someone being a successful leader in their school. They liked it better when people turned to them for advice. They may well have serious emotional problems that feed their destructive tendencies (Zey, 1990, pp. 134-139).

What Are the Dirty Dozen School Sicknesses?

With sincere apologies to medical professionals everywhere and especially to those among the readers who may have first-hand (and very painful) knowledge of these ailments, I offer the following tongue-in-cheek compendium of "illnesses" that can attack and de-bilitate the typical school from within.

1. Paralysis

The symptoms of "paralysis" in a school are seen largely in the inability of anyone to get anything done. Sometimes, the paralysis is the result of an administrator who makes all the decisions. He or she holds such a tight rein on the organization that no one can do any-thing unless the administrator decrees it. This behavior forces staff members to put a lid on creativity because good ideas never go any-where but into the circular file. This kind of paralysis results in a malaise of inaction and uncertainty.

2. Diarrhea

The principal symptom of "diarrhea" in the school setting is a constant flow of aggressive and abusive words and actions from par-ents, students, teachers, staff members, and administrators. Oh, there may be a few thoughtful or sweet-tempered souls somewhere in the bunch, but they will soon learn how business is done and get into line to vent along with everyone else. The symptoms of this kind of diarrhea are frequently evidenced by outbursts in public places, swearing, and an occasional show of physical violence.

3. Chronic Fatigue

When everyone wants somebody else to do something and no one is willing to step up and roll up (their sleeves, that is), "chronic fatigue" has set in. This problem could be caused by overwork and burnout, lack of leadership and motivation, or the absence of a meaningful mission and vision. The disease is debilitating, and sym-pathetic reactions often make it seem more widespread. Boredom and depression often accompany the fatigue, and a feeling of hope-lessness may also set in.

4. Hypertension

Hypertension in the body is often described as a heart attack or stroke waiting to happen. "Hypertension" in a school setting is somewhat akin, much like a pot that is about ready to boil over. There are lots of fights on the playground, tension in the teachers' lounge, and wrinkled brows in the main office. Everyone feels uneasy, but they aren't sure just why. Griping and complaining are acute. Before long, Mt. Vesuvius will erupt, and all hell will break loose. By then, major damage will have been done, and repair is difficult and costly.

5. Heart Failure

The symptoms of "heart failure" are lack of empathy, understanding, and caring. Everyone wants to be heard and understood. No one is willing to "walk a mile in another's moccasins," and a frequently heard aphorism is "I'm looking out for Number 1."

6. Lockjaw

"Lockjaw" results in the inability of people to talk to one another about what's really on their minds. Problems are swept under the rug, or they are discussed in informal "parking lot meetings" but never in public or in an organized fashion. The administrator is the key carrier of this kind of lockjaw, and its spread can be epidemic if his or her case is a particularly virulent one.

7. Circulatory Collapse

The decline of appropriate two-way communication channels signals an imminent "circulatory collapse." When information isn't moving clearly and consistently among and between all the participants in the life of a school, circulatory collapse has occurred. This disease is exacerbated by gossip and can be fatal if left untreated.

8. Muscle and Tendon Inflammation

This condition is annoying and pervasive. "Muscle and tendon inflammation" is characterized by intermittent bouts of aggressive and hostile interpersonal communication. What causes or exacerbates this kind of inflammation is frequently a source of consternation to the participants. "What set her off?" "I have no idea what's bothering him." "Do you think it was something I said or did?" Just when you're planning for smooth sailing ahead, inflammation will flare up, creating irritability, a decline in self-esteem, and extreme frustration.

9. Irritable Bowel Syndrome

The principal symptom of this kind of "irritable bowel syndrome" is the presence of chronic complaining and criticism. No matter what anyone does, it's never enough, and it's always wrong. Both apologies and compliments are greeted with disdain, and most irritable-bowel sufferers order T-shirts with one of two mottoes emblazoned on the front: "The glass is half-empty" or "The sky is falling."

10. Calluses, Corns, and Bunions

The toughness and misshapenness that characterize real-life calluses, corns, and bunions can also be found in the close-mindedness and rigidity of this affliction in the school setting. The inability to soften, relent, give in, or fit in when seen in a critical mass of faculty, parents, and children will result in the inability of the school to adopt a new paradigm, restructure, or reform.

11. Chicken Pox

When seen in the school setting, this common childhood disease takes a slightly different form. The emphasis is on the "chicken" rather than the "pox," its principal symptom being an unreasonable fear of taking a position or providing leadership. This is another one of those diseases that relies on a carrier to expose others to the virus; the administrator is particularly susceptible and can unwittingly infect an entire school population.

12. Malnutrition

This malady is difficult to diagnose and in its early stages, impossible to recognize. It can afflict staff members who don't seek advanced degrees or who sneer at staff development. It can be seen in a watered-down curriculum with low expectations for students. Even the administrator is prone to this kind of malnutrition by thinking that teaching and learning are only for the teachers and kids. The results of educational malnutrition are poor student achievement, low teacher morale and efficacy, and rampant parental dissatisfaction.

Does Your School Have a Fever?

If your body has a temperature, that's a signal that you're fighting off an infection. There are also ways to take your school's temperature to see if it's fighting off a microbe invasion of dissatisfaction, distrust, and disorganization. If the mercury is rising, treatment could be needed. Use the following checklist (McEwan, 1997a, pp. 61-63, 1997b, pp. 151-179) to determine the status of your school's health.

How Healthy Is Your School?

Instructions: Circle the number of the descriptor that best describes the behavior of individuals in your school. When you have completed all 16 indicators, add up your total score and see how you rate.

Score	Rating
71-80	Superior Health. Continue to do all of the good things you're doing, and monitor vital signs daily.
61-70	Excellent Health. Even though you're in good shape, don't grow complacent.
51-60	Good Health. With some fine-tuning in several areas, you could be much healthier than you are.
41-50	Poor Health. One more crisis and you'll be hospitalized. Change your lifestyle.
40 and Under	Intensive care! No visitors until further notice!

Indicator 1: *All students are treated with respect by all staff members (principal, teachers, secretary, custodial staff, bus drivers, cafeteria workers, etc.).*

Scale of Descriptors:

1. There is an overall feeling on the part of most staff members that students are out of control. Some staff members resort to yelling, "getting physical," sarcasm, and meaningless punishments. There are frequent power struggles between students and adult staff members. Other staff members tend to ignore and demean students by ignoring problems. Staff members frequently complain about student behavior, a favorite topic of discussion in the teachers' lounge.

2. Although some staff members genuinely respect students and are proactive with regard to troublesome student behavior, they are in the minority. Most teachers feel powerless to change student behavior and treat students with a critical and mean-spirited attitude.

3. Many staff members behave positively and respectfully toward students but are reluctant to defend students or offer positive solutions in the face of their more pessimistic colleagues.

4. Although most staff members behave positively and respectfully toward students, there are several pockets of resistance and negativism on the part of teachers.

5. All staff members feel positively and act respectfully toward all students, even those who are challenging. When difficulties arise, they handle them through appropriate channels (e.g., Teacher Assistance Team, referral, consultation with principal, etc.).

Indicator 2: *The principal and staff establish high expectations for student achievement, which are directly communicated to students and parents.*

Scale of Descriptors:

1. Principal and staff believe that nonalterable variables, such as home background, socioeconomic status, and ability level, are the prime determinants of student achievement and that the school cannot overcome these factors.

2. Principal and staff believe that the nonalterable variables cited earlier significantly affect student achievement and the school has a limited impact on student achievement.

3. Principal and staff believe that although the nonalterable variables cited earlier may influence student achievement, teachers are responsible for all students mastering basic skills or prescribed learner outcomes according to individual levels of expectancy. The principal occasionally communicates these expectations in an informal way to teachers, parents, and students via written and spoken communications, specific activities, or a combination of these.

4. Principal and staff believe that although the nonalterable variables cited earlier may influence student achievement, teachers are responsible for all students mastering certain basic skills at their grade level and frequently communicate these expectations to parents and students in a formal, organized manner. Expectations for student achievement may be communicated through written statements of objectives in basic skills, written statements of purpose or mission for the school that guides the instructional program, or both.

5. Principal and staff believe that together the home and school can have a profound influence on student achievement. Teachers are held responsible not only for all students mastering certain basic skills at their grade levels but for the stimulation, enrichment, and acceleration of the students who are able to learn more quickly and the provision of extended learning opportunities for students who may need more time for mastery. Expectations for student achievement are developed jointly among parent, student, and teacher and are communicated not only through written statements of learner outcomes in core curriculum areas but in enriched and accelerated programs, achievement awards, and opportunities for creative expression.

Indicator 3: *Principal and staff members serve as advocates of students and communicate with them regarding aspects of their school life.* Behaviors might include lunch with individual students or groups; frequent appearances on the playground, in the lunchroom, and in the hallways; sponsorship of clubs, availability to students who wish to discuss instructional or disciplinary concerns; knowledge of students' names (other than just your own classes) and family relationships, addressing the majority of students by name; and willingness to listen to the students' side in faculty-student problems. The preceding list is meant only to be suggestive of the type of behaviors that might be appropriate for consideration in this category.

Scale of Descriptors:

1. Principal and staff do not feel that acting as student advocates is an appropriate role and never interact with students on this basis.

2. Principal and staff feel that acting as student advocates is an appropriate role but feel uncomfortable and rarely do it. They seldom interact with students on this basis.

3. Principal and staff rarely act as student advocates but engage in at least three behaviors that encourage communication.

4. Principal and staff feel that acting as student advocates is an appropriate role and engage in at least six behaviors that encourage communication.

5. Principal and staff feel that acting as student advocates is an appropriate role and engage in at least six behaviors that encourage communication as well as establishing some means of receiving input from students regarding their opinions of school and classroom life.

Indicator 4: *Principal encourages open communication among staff members and parents and maintains respect for differences of opinion.* The main focus of this indicator is on the behaviors that the principal exhibits that give evidence of maintenance of open communication among staff members and parents and respect for differences of opinion. Behaviors might include an open-door policy in the principal's office, acceptance of unpopular ideas and negative feedback from staff and parents, provision of channels for staff and parents to voice grievances or discuss problems, and provision of channels for staff members and parents to interact with each other. The preceding list is meant only to be suggestive of the type of behaviors that might be appropriate for consideration in this category.

Scale of Descriptors:

1. Principal does not encourage open communication among staff members and parents and considers differences of opinion to be a sign of disharmony among organizational members.

2. Principal supports open communication but is rarely available for informal encounters with staff members or parents. Appointments must be scheduled, meeting agendas are tightly maintained, and the flow of information and opinions is artificially controlled.

3. Principal supports open communication and is available for informal encounters with staff members and parents. Prin-

cipal is not responsive, however, to problems, questions, or disagreements and shuts off communication of this nature.

4. Principal supports open communication and is available for informal encounters with staff members and parents. Principal is responsive to problems, questions, or disagreements and encourages staff members and parents to work through differences of opinion in positive ways.

5. Principal supports open communication and is available for informal encounters with staff members and parents. An open-door policy exists with regard to all problems, questions, and disagreements. Principal structures a variety of opportunities for staff members and parents to interact both formally and informally, encouraging interaction among grade levels, departments, and instructional teams.

Indicator 5: Principal demonstrates concern and openness in the consideration of teacher, parent, or student problems and participates in the resolution of such problems where appropriate.

Scale of Descriptors:

1. Principal does not wish to be involved in the consideration of teacher, parent, or student problems.

2. Principal is willing to be involved in the consideration of teacher, parent, or student problems but is largely ineffective because of poor communication and human relations skills.

3. Principal is willing to be involved in the consideration of teacher, parent, or student problems and is sometimes effective in bringing problems to resolution. Exhibits average communication and human relations skills.

4. Principal is willing to be involved in the consideration of teacher, parent, or student problems and is usually effective in bringing problems to resolution. Exhibits excellent communication and human relations skills.

5. Principal is willing to be involved in the consideration of teacher, parent, or student problems and is nearly always effective in bringing problems to resolution. Exhibits outstanding communication and human relations skills. Has estab-

lished procedures jointly with faculty for the resolution of problems.

Indicator 6: Principal models appropriate human relations skills. The main focus of this indicator is the variety of appropriate human relations skills that are exhibited by the principal. Behaviors must include, but not necessarily be limited to, (a) establishing a climate of trust and security for students and staff; (b) respecting the rights of students, parents, and staff; (c) handling individual relationships tactfully and with understanding; and (d) accepting the dignity and worth of individuals without regard to appearance, race, creed, sex, disability, ability, or social status.

Scale of Descriptors:

1. Principal exhibits none of the behaviors described.
2. Principal exhibits only one or two of the behaviors described and often has difficulty with tasks that involve human interaction.
3. Principal exhibits two or three of the behaviors described and is usually successful with tasks that involve human interaction.
4. Principal exhibits three or four of the behaviors described and is frequently successful with tasks that involve human interaction.
5. Principal exhibits all of the behaviors described as well as many other behaviors associated with good human relations and is almost always successful with tasks that involve human interaction.

Indicator 7: Principal develops and maintains high morale. The main focus of this indicator is the variety of behaviors exhibited by the principal that contribute to the development and maintenance of high morale. Behaviors might include but are not necessarily limited to involvement of staff in planning, encouragement of planned social events, openness in the dissemination of information, equity in the division of responsibility and allocation of resources, opportunities for achievement, recognition for achievements, involvement of the staff in problem solving, and assistance and support with personal and professional problems.

Scale of Descriptors:

1. Morale is nonexistent in the school building. Principal exhibits none of the behaviors described earlier. There is little unity among staff members, leading to competition, clique formation, destructive criticism, disagreement, and verbal quarreling.
2. Morale is marginal in the school building. Principal exhibits few of the behaviors described. Although fewer visible signs of disunity are evident, faculty members nevertheless do not work well together or have positive feelings about their work.
3. Morale is average. Although there are no visible signs of disunity as seen in Descriptor 1, teachers work largely as individuals, rarely working together cooperatively with enthusiasm and positive feelings.
4. Morale is excellent. Morale-building behaviors by the principal result in teachers working together to share ideas and resources, to identify instructional problems, to define mutual goals, and to coordinate their activities.
5. Morale is outstanding. Morale-building behaviors by the principal result in teachers working together in a highly effective way while gaining personal satisfaction from their work. Principal has identified specific activities that build morale and systematically engages in these activities.

Indicator 8: *Principal systematically collects and responds to staff, parent, and student concerns.* The main focus of this indicator is the responsiveness of the principal to the concerns of staff, parents, and students that have been systematically collected. Examples of vehicles used to collect information might include, but are not necessarily limited to, one-on-one conferences, parent or faculty advisory committees, student council, suggestion boxes, or quality circles.

Scale of Descriptors:

1. No information is collected from staff, parents, and students. Principal is unresponsive to concerns of these groups.
2. Although information is sporadically collected from groups, principal is largely ineffective in responding to concerns.

3. Information is systematically collected from at least one of the three groups, and the principal is effective in responding to concerns.

4. Information is systematically collected from at least two of the three groups, and the principal is effective in responding to concerns.

5. Information is systematically collected from parents, faculty, and students; principal is effective in responding to concerns; and information is used in planning and implementing change.

Indicator 9: Principal appropriately acknowledges the earned achievements of others. The main focus of this indicator is the variety of activities engaged in by the principal that demonstrate the ability to recognize the contributions of staff, students, and parents. Activities might include, but are not necessarily limited to, staff recognition programs, student award assemblies, certificates, congratulatory notes, phone calls, recognition luncheons, and newspaper articles.

Scale of Descriptors:

1. Principal engages in no recognition activities.
2. Principal engages in at least one recognition activity for one of the three groups (staff, parents, students).
3. Principal engages in at least one recognition activity for two of the three groups (staff, parents, students).
4. Principal engages in at least one recognition activity for all three groups (staff, parents, students).
5. In addition to a variety of recognition activities, the principal involves all three groups in recognition activities for one another.

Indicator 10: All staff members (classified and certified) are able to communicate openly with one another and say what they feel.

Scale of Descriptors:

1. Discussion is inhibited and stilted. People are hesitant to lay their true feelings on the table and are afraid of criticism, putdowns, and reprisals.

2. A few self-confident or politically connected people speak openly, but most are reluctant.

3. Many staff members speak openly but usually only after a communication trend has been established.

4. Although most communication is open, there are some topics that are taboo, or select individuals inhibit open communication with what they say or do.

5. Discussion is always free-wheeling and frank. There is no hesitation on the part of all staff members to "tell it like it is," even in high-risk discussions and decision making. Staff members feel free to express their feelings as well as their ideas.

Indicator 11: *The individual abilities, knowledge, and experience of all staff members are fully used.*

Scale of Descriptors:

1. The staff is controlled by one individual who runs the show.

2. A select and chosen few do all the work.

3. At least half of the staff do something, but the same people are always in charge.

4. A majority of the staff participates by doing something, but no effort is made to share or exchange roles.

5. All staff members are recognized as having gifts and talents that are fully used in accomplishing building goals, and roles are shared and exchanged.

Indicator 12: *Conflict between various individuals (teachers, parents, students) is resolved openly and effectively, and there is a genuine feeling of respect for one another among these groups.*

Scale of Descriptors:

1. People suppress conflict and pretend it does not exist.

2. People recognize conflict but do not approach its solution directly and positively.

3. People recognize conflict and attempt to resolve it with some success, but they are sometimes clumsy and unskilled in their methodology, resulting in frequent misunderstandings.

4. People recognize conflict and can frequently resolve it through appropriate methods, but there are no standardized methodologies for handling conflict.

5. People are skilled at recognizing conflict and have a variety of conflict resolution strategies in their repertoire that they use with great success.

Indicator 13: *The entire school community can articulate and is committed to the vision and mission of the school.*

Scale of Descriptors:

1. People are openly committed to their own agendas and are unwilling to set aside personal goals for the school mission.

2. People pretend to be committed to the mission but frequently work at cross-purposes.

3. A core of people (staff and parents) are committed, but a few naysayers and bystanders often work to undermine the mission when it serves their purposes.

4. The majority of people are committed, but no intentional efforts have been made to work through any existing group differences.

5. People have worked through their differences, and they can honestly say they are committed to achieving the mission of the school.

Indicator 14: *Staff members can express their views openly without fear of ridicule or retaliation and let others do the same.*

Scale of Descriptors:

1. Staff members never express views openly.

2. Some staff members express views openly, but it is usually done with hesitancy and reluctance.

3. Some staff members feel free to express views openly, but many members are reluctant to express their true feelings.

4. Constructive criticism is accepted, but there are no mechanisms for ensuring that it is a regular aspect of teamwork.

5. Constructive criticism is frequent, frank, and two-way; staff members accept and encourage it. Group processes are used that intentionally monitor and encourage the free flow of opinions, ideas, and suggestions for improvement.

Indicator 15: *Staff members can get help from one another and give help without being concerned about hidden agendas.*

Scale of Descriptors:

1. Staff members are reluctant to admit ignorance or the need for assistance. They are in the "independent" rather than "interdependent" modes.

2. Some staff members will admit to the need for assistance, but many are territorial and competitive.

3. Staff members want to be cooperative but lack the necessary skills.

4. Staff members assist each other, but there is no systematic plan for evaluating the effectiveness of the cooperative atmosphere.

5. Staff members have no reluctance in asking for help from others or in offering help to fellow staff members. There is transparency and trust among staff members. Processes are used regularly to examine how well the staff is working together and what may be interfering with its cooperation.

Indicator 16: *The school climate is one of openness and respect for individual differences.*

Scale of Descriptors:

1. Parents and staff members are suspicious and disrespectful of one another.

2. A few parents and staff members are trying to improve the climate but are having a difficult time bringing about change.

3. The majority of parents and teachers work well together, but there are some who attempt to undermine a healthy climate.

4. Parents and staff work well together, but little is done to encourage, develop, and affirm this sense of teamwork.

5. Parents and staff respect and affirm the unique gifts and talents of each individual with appreciation for the variety of learning styles, personalities, and intelligences.

What Does a Healthy School Look Like?

Are you beginning to get the idea of what a healthy school looks like? When you're trying to nurture a healthy school, you have to know what a good one looks like. The physician who is examining cells under the microscope to determine if disease is present must have a clear picture of healthy cells in mind before he or she can diagnose sickness. There are several key principles of a healthy school that seem to sum up rather nicely the qualities and characteristics described in the Healthy School Checklist (Steinke, 1996). These generalizations have applicability to each of the distinct groups of people who live and work in the school community: parents, students, certified staff, classified staff, and administrators.

Mission and Vision

The healthy school is a purposeful one. There is a clear vision for the future and an immediate mission for tomorrow. There are places to go and things to do, and everyone agrees on what they are.

Separate yet Connected

The individuals in a healthy school are separate yet connected. Let me explain. In any type of relationship there are two very unhealthy opposite ends of a continuum—the point at which individuals are so intent on having their own way with no compromise that dissolution (or divorce) is the only alternative, or the equally distressing opposite point, fusion, where there is no room for any individual freedom, and everyone must think and speak the "party line." Healthy relationships in schools, like healthy marriage relationships, are characterized by a separateness that allows for differences and dialogues as well as a connectedness that encourages collaboration and consensus. The extremes of fusion and dissolution are equally unhealthy.

Leaders who insist on cloning themselves when hiring faculty or who are only happy when everyone agrees with everything they do are creating a very unhealthy environment for both themselves and staff members.

Metanoia Rather Than Paranoia

Metanoia and *paranoia* are Greek words referring to states of mind. Metanoia literally means "repentance" or the ability to change one's mind. People with this quality are able to take responsibility for their actions and assume ownership for the impact their inappropriate behaviors may have on others. They do not carry the baggage of anger and grudges forward to each new day. They are able to forgive and forget. In contrast, the individual with paranoia (literally, the state of being out of one's mind) is out of control. He or she is unable to regulate his or her behavior and lacks a clear definition of self. Whereas paranoia is a bona fide mental disorder, there are many educators and parents who live in a borderline state of suspicion, criticism, and blame. Too many of these folks on your staff or in your parent community can make for an unhealthy school.

Optimism Rather Than Pessimism

In a healthy school, people feel empowered to solve problems, meet challenges, and overcome adversity. This attitude is fostered by shared decision making; individual and group accountability; and the provision of resources, both human and material. The healthy school can heal itself and bounce back from adversity, a natural aspect of organizational growth and change.

Cooperation Rather Than Competition

Cooperation and interdependence are fostered, rather than competition. Teachers keep their doors open, share ideas and materials, and are able to ask for help in solving problems. Most school staffs still have a long way to go in their understanding of teamwork; they don't really believe that they need each other to accomplish a result. Teachers have traditionally been able to shut their doors and do what they do in privacy, and when all is said and done, they are much more comfortable in this role than in working together. But if all the staff members are responsible for all of the children and are held accountable for the "graduates" of each school (elementary, middle, high school), teachers must begin to look at teamwork in a completely different light.

Zero Tolerance of Intolerance

A healthy school is caring and compassionate. Meanness, sarcasm, prejudice, and bitterness are identified, discussed, and eliminated. All members of the school community must hear and heed the same message (teachers hear it from administrators, kids hear it from teachers), and anything less than zero tolerance is not tolerated.

Maturity and Growth

The healthy school invests time and money in learning for everyone: students, teachers, parents. The leader doesn't protect or rescue people but enables and empowers them. The learning environment I refer to is different from the "book learning" we traditionally associate with school—studying, memorizing, and taking tests. "It starts with self-mastery and self-knowledge, but involves looking outward to develop knowledge of, and alignment with, others on your team" (Roberts, 1994, p. 355).

What Does a Healthy Leader Look Like?

The healthy leader is ready to accept a challenge, is flexible, is willing to consider many options, and is able to leap tall buildings in a single bound. Seriously, being a genuine leader calls for strong emotional, physical, mental, and spiritual health. Healthy leadership provides a strong immune system for a school. The healthy leader must have the ability to follow this advice from Hamlet: "To thine own self be true; And it must follow, as the night the day, Thou canst not then be false to any man" (Shakespeare, *Hamlet*, act I, scene iii). The healthy leader has the following characteristics (Steinke, 1996, p. 98):

- Is able to take a position based on values, principles, and beliefs
- Is aware of personal emotions
- Can manage anxiety
- Can manage anger
- Is able to make adjustments in behavior and feelings
- Stays connected to others
- Recognizes and can deal with emotions in others
- Tolerates differences
- Encourages dialogue
- Defines self from within
- Lives with a purpose in mind
- Moves forward
- Stretches and grows
- Is ready for and can cope with the "pain" that comes with leading

What Can Be Done to Promote and Maintain a Healthy School?

The maintenance of a healthy body is a somewhat tedious and often monotonous job requiring time, discipline, and steadiness. Exercising, flossing (something that I personally despise), taking vitamins and minerals, and eating a healthy diet are practices that many of us do sporadically, if at all. Oh, we have bursts of good intentions, but they frequently fall by the wayside under time constraints or sheer boredom. Eventually, however (for some, sooner rather than later), our neglect and carelessness will result in disease (whether it's our gums, our heart, or our bones), and we will find ourselves facing the painful reality that we have unalterably damaged our bodies.

Reread the Healthy School Checklist for specific ideas, and consider the following suggestions as well:

- Hire staff who are emotionally healthy. Pay attention during the interview process to the emotional health of your candidates. A secretary who can type 150 words per minute and knows every software program in the book but can't empathize with teachers, parents, and students will be worthless. The teacher who graduated Phi Beta Kappa but isn't willing to cooperate with the grade level team on an interdisciplinary unit will be a liability.

- Tend to your own emotional health. If you're out of control, build time in your daily calendar for exercise, "down time," and lunch. Seek professional help if you find yourself becoming angry, reactive, and unable to respond in appropriate ways.

- Just as the mechanic lowers the dipstick into your engine's crankcase to check the oil level, "dipstick" your school occasionally to see how things are going. Talk to parents, teachers, and students. Send out surveys, or form focus groups. Don't be the last to know that trouble is brewing.

- Share information. A well-informed and knowledgeable staff is more likely to work together. Don't keep people in the dark about important decisions.

- Share the glory. When staff members can work together and share the credit for accomplishments, an organization gains vitality and energy.

- Schedule staff development activities that focus on team building, cooperative learning, conflict resolution, and other topics that force individuals to consider their individual behavior as it affects the school's mission.

- Reward honesty and transparency. When staff members are willing to bring difficult issues out in the open and deal with them, an atmosphere of trust will develop that can help weather times of stress.

What Steps Can You Take If Your School Is Ill?

If after reading this chapter you feel that your school may be ill, there are several things you can and should do. Do remember, however, that your school is a system, and you can't isolate or tinker with one thing without affecting all of the other parts of the system. Here are some suggestions:

- Ask the staff, parents, and students what they think is wrong. Use group processes, such as the Force Field Analysis (McEwan, 1997a, pp. 100-101) or the Apollo Process (McEwan, 1997a, pp. 117-118), to identify specific problems that are keeping your school from achieving health.

- Develop a school mission statement. If you don't know where you're going, chances are you won't get there. The development of a mission statement can bring focus and direction to a group.

- Take steps to get rid of staff members who are causing problems. If a problem is really serious (incompetent, ineffective teaching), follow the due-process remediation and dismissal plan that is part of your negotiated contract. If the problem is less well-defined but nevertheless troublesome, consider an involuntary transfer. A change of scenery can often shake up a whiner or wake up a late bloomer.

- Hire a consultant to conduct an audit. People will often be more honest with an outsider, and an objective professional can diagnose the problem in a relatively short period of time. This exercise will be worth every penny you spend.

5

The Proactive Approach: Fifty Ways to Build Parental Support for Your School

> Collaboration is strengthened through weaving the web of personal relationships. Community builders recognize that, as human beings, we need the opportunity to respond personally to each other, and, as importantly, to feel known and "seen" as valued community contributors.
>
> —Juanita Brown and David Isaacs (Brown & Isaacs, 1994, p. 516)

Developing solid home-school partnerships is important for lots of reasons. Here are just a few:

- Students are more successful in school when their parents and school personnel work closely and cooperatively.

- Parents will be more supportive and willing to give educators the benefit of the doubt, even in stress-filled and emotional encounters, when there is a history of working together.

- Everyone in the schooling business (parents, teachers, administrators, and students) will benefit from two-way information sharing and collaborative problem solving.

Build a strong base of parental involvement and support in your school by becoming a proactive principal.

Fifty Suggestions to Get You Started

1. Shared Decision Making

Involve parents in a site-based decision-making group. Many teachers and administrators are wary of inviting parents to sit in on heated discussions about school improvement, but if you provide training and support, you won't be sorry.

Too often, we make decisions that will affect our parent community without ever bothering to ask for its input. Or worse, we ask for it and don't use it.

2. Management by Walking Around

Keep your antennae waving as you meet with parents. Ask people what they're thinking, how they're feeling, and how their children are doing. Monitor your parents through surveys, phone polls, asking questions, and having an open-door policy. You can detect subtle trends, pick up on a snowballing problem, or even receive an unsolicited compliment if you tune in to the informal parent network.

3. Think Ahead

Learn to anticipate problems before they arise. Stay abreast of the education news and do your homework. If you have anticipated a controversial issue and developed policies and procedures in advance of parental concerns, you'll come across as more competent and credible.

4. Key Communicators

Some of the most influential communicators regarding your school are the classified staff. If you're implementing a new program, explain it to bus drivers, crossing guards, cafeteria workers, secretaries, and maintenance staff. They wield considerable influence in the community, and their conversations in grocery stores, barber shops, and the corner diner will help to shape parental and public opinion of your school (for good or ill).

5. Advance Warning

If you're going to make a change at your school, even if it's something as minor (to you) as the direction in which the cars move in the traffic circle, give parents lots of warning. Changing things such as lunch schedules, report cards, course offerings, sports eligibility rules, immunization requirements, or transportation schedules without warning (and sometimes, even with) can put parents in an uproar.

6. A Key Decision-Making Tool

A key tool in making decisions is a well-timed meeting. If you don't have an answer, ask for time to do research; then schedule another meeting. Give parents the sense that when decisions are made, they're not made in haste. Even if you don't give them what they want, please consider their input carefully. You may just find yourself changing your mind.

7. Single Parents

Recognize the special needs of single-parent families. Be willing to set aside your traditional notions of a "good" family to benefit children who are being raised in more "contemporary" families. Provide child care for social events and parent-teacher conferences so that single parents can more easily attend.

8. Breaking Up Is Hard to Do

Accommodating the needs of divorced parents often means going out of your way to provide dual report cards and separate parent-teacher conferences, but the payback in good will and support for a child already torn between mom and dad is worth it. Some districts are even willing to ease residency rules while families are in transition. That, of course, is a matter of policy.

9. Multicultural Outreach

Understanding the cultural contexts of students and families is especially important for building strong school-family bonds. Be sensitive to nonverbal communication cues, such as eye contact, personal space, and personal touch. Enlist the help of community and religious leaders to build bridges with the cultural or ethnic minorities in your attendance area.

10. Home Visits

If your budget and teachers' contract restraints permit, schedule time for home visits, even if only at a few grade levels. If a home visit doesn't seem practical, parents and teachers can meet on more neutral ground, such as the parent's workplace or a restaurant.

11. Good News Travels Fast

Develop a culture in your school that supports, encourages, and even expects a continued staff outreach to parents through home visits, weekly or periodic newsletters, and positive telephone calls.

12. Read All About It

Publish a schoolwide newsletter that contains articles by and about teachers, students, and parents. The principal should regularly contribute a letter or column, and the focus should always be positive. I personally wrote a weekly question-and-answer column for our community newspaper, which was a perfect vehicle for answering parents' questions as well as those from the public.

13. Let's Party

Plan social gatherings that permit parents, educators, and students to be with each other in informal ways. Possibilities include back-to-school events, such as picnics and potlucks, ethnic celebrations and dances, welcoming gatherings for new students and parents (e.g., kindergarten, beginning of middle and high school). Holiday breakfasts and events for grandparents or other family members are also marvelous opportunities for strengthening the home-school connection.

14. Put Out the Welcome Mat

Make your school an inviting place to visit. Provide signs that welcome visitors and point them to the office. Create an atmosphere where teachers, students, and other staff members routinely greet school visitors and ask if they can help them. If languages other than

English are spoken by parents, make sure that someone is always available to translate. Display student artwork and other class projects to communicate the emphasis on learning that is present in your building.

15. Open House

In addition to social events and informal gatherings, plan regular open-house events to communicate important information about curriculum and to show off student work. Science fairs, art shows, young authors' conferences, and musical concerts give students an opportunity to shine.

16. Curricular Expectations

What do you expect students to know and be able to do when they exit each grade level in your school (kindergarten through 12th grade)? How well have you communicated that information to parents? Consider publishing a booklet that sets forth the expectations for each grade level or course to let parents know the mission of your school.

17. Read to Me

Open the school library during evening hours for "study hall" or for family story hours. Encourage parents to check out books for their children or for their own personal use.

18. Kudos to Volunteers

Recognize and reward the many parent volunteers who work in your school with their own personalized T-shirt, a yearly luncheon, or recognition in the school newsletter.

19. Teacher Training

Provide training for your staff in how to communicate with parents, how to handle parents who are upset, and how to answer questions parents have about student problems, curriculum, and school policies. Uninformed teachers are public relations disasters waiting to happen. Don't take for granted the abilities of your teachers to use tact, discretion, and common sense in parental encounters. Schedule a staff development session now.

20. *The Night Shift*

Be sensitive to the needs of dual-career families and unique work demands when you schedule parent-teacher conferences or special events. Alternate yearly musical programs between afternoon and evening performances to give everyone a chance to attend once in awhile. Schedule evening parent-teacher conferences also.

21. *School-Business Partnerships*

Team up with local businesses in partnerships. Our school teamed up with an international seed company with headquarters in our attendance area. Certain grade levels took field trips there each year, and students had the opportunity to see their parents at work. Personnel from the company also worked with our teachers to develop research projects in horticulture.

22. *Phone Home*

Install telephones in teachers' classrooms so they can easily phone parents and parents can reach them. Be sure to include a voice mail option so that incoming calls that arrive during classroom instruction will not disturb the class. Professionals in most businesses have their own phone lines, and this provision for teachers eliminates lost messages and secretarial gridlock.

23. *The Dog Ate It*

Install a homework hot line where students and parents can verify homework assignments. The same system can also accommodate absentee calls and include a calendar of upcoming events.

24. *Keyboard Capers*

Solicit donations of used computers and make them available to families in your community for a weekly or monthly checkout period. Students who have received training at school will provide the support that's needed at home.

25. The Family That Learns Together

Schedule family math and science nights where parents and students attend together and do hands-on activities. This is a perfect way to introduce parents to a new curriculum or methodology and to build in "quality time" for families. Be sure to provide child care for very small children.

26. School-Community Partnerships

Initiatives such as Drug-Free Schools programs, Neighborhood Helping Hands, Neighborhood Watch, and other crime prevention programs offer perfect opportunities for educators, parents, and community officials (police, fire, municipal governments) to work together.

27. Parents as Teachers

Offer workshops for parents (e.g., how to help children become better readers, or how to structure a discipline plan at home). Enlist the help of your school psychologist, behavior management specialist, social worker, and others to conduct the training.

28. Career Days

Invite parents to classrooms to talk about their careers. Encourage them to bring along several items they use in their work and to come in their work clothing. Another event that will bring parents (and other relatives) to school is the opportunity to read their favorite story aloud in a classroom.

29. Habla Español?

Provide important materials to parents in their native language. Whenever possible, report cards, handbooks, notices of meetings, and all special education documents should be published in the languages spoken by the parents of your students.

30. Speak to Me

Provide translators at important meetings that involve individual students as well as for schoolwide meetings, such as PTA or Home-School Council.

31. *The Cable Connection*

Use your local-access cable TV station to communicate with parents. One principal I know has a monthly Fireside Chat program and another regularly reads stories aloud via TV. Broadcasting musical concerts and school plays enables parents to enjoy school events if their schedules have kept them from attending.

32. *Put Your Money Where Your Mouth Is*

If your budget permits, hire a parent liaison or home-school coordinator. This individual can make home visits, conduct parent education classes, and create goodwill in the community.

33. *Computer Literacy*

Hold a computer course for parents in your school's computer lab. Hire one of your staff members to teach the course.

34. *Berlitz Comes to School*

If other languages are spoken in your school, offer language classes for credit so that more staff members will be able to communicate with parents. Although fluency in a foreign language is a goal that takes some time to achieve, even the smallest gestures of staff members toward communication will be noted and appreciated by parents.

35. *A Solid Foundation*

Form an educational foundation to enlist the help of parents and community members in raising funds for projects such as minigrants to teachers, scholarships to summer enrichment programs for students, and technology centers.

36. *What's the Score?*

Hold a yearly meeting to discuss and explain test scores to parents. Invite a representative from a local college or university to your high school to talk about admission requirements and how test scores are used. Or have a representative from the testing company available to talk to parents who want more detailed explanations of statistics.

37. *Can We Talk?*

Hold regularly scheduled parent conferences (twice yearly is preferable) at which student progress is discussed and learning goals for the future are formulated.

38. *Preferred Parking*

Provide special parking places for parents who visit the building to volunteer or meet with staff. There's nothing more frustrating to parents than having to park miles away from the building or worry about getting a parking ticket.

39. *When I Want Your Advice, I'll Ask For It*

Form an advisory council that is kept apprised of everything that is happening at school and in turn feeds back suggestions and questions from the school community. Well-trained advisory council members can keep communication flowing and help to quash rumors and untruths.

40. *Here's How to Handle a Problem*

Publish a "what to do if you have a problem at school" booklet, letting parents know the procedures to follow for solving specific problems and what to expect in the way of help.

41. *Plan Ahead*

Publish a yearly school calendar that contains information about all of the important events to take place in the year (athletic contests, musical concerts, fund-raising events, beginning and end of marking periods, etc.) Your staff (and parent leaders) will complain the first time you ask them to choose all of their dates a year in advance, but the calendar will help parents plan ahead. Nothing makes parents madder than last-minute schedule changes or event announcements that go astray.

42. *Rules of the Road*

Publish a school handbook with all the rules, regulations, and information parents and students need to "survive" in your school.

Although there are no guarantees that everyone will read what you publish, at least you gave them the opportunity.

43. Talk to Me

Cultivate a communication culture in which teachers are sensitive to the need for immediate communication when student problems arise. Educators have a responsibility to let parents know immediately of inappropriate behavior, missed assignments, class cutting, and so forth.

44. Paid Parents

When you have the opportunity to hire parents in your school and they have the qualifications you need, don't hesitate to do so. You will need to provide training and clear expectations regarding their responsibilities to be discrete, but a loyal parent employee will work twice as hard at a job in their child's school than they would anywhere else.

45. The Volunteer Army

Structure a variety of volunteer opportunities in your school. Don't assume that parents of middle school or high school students won't volunteer. You may not get as many of them as elementary administrators got when their children were in kindergarten, but have you asked?

46. Pop the Question

Take every opportunity you have to talk to parents about their children. They have information we need to know, information that can help us do a better job of educating their children. And when parents talk, listen.

47. Reach Out and Touch Someone

I am aware of the pervasive popularity of automated telephone systems with elaborate options. However, when parents call the school (other than to leave a message on a teacher's voice mail), they usually want to speak to someone. Make sure that whoever is answering your school phone is well trained and projects a positive image. This individual should have information at his or her finger-tips regarding special events, knowledge about upcoming field trips, and know the whereabouts of key people (administrators, school nurse, psychologist, etc.). Parents who leave messages for the princi-pal would find it helpful to know that he or she is out of town and will not be getting the message for a period of time. If the necessary evil of voice mail has arrived in your school, instruct staff members to change their reply message to coordinate with their schedules. I find it most helpful to know whether someone is in or out of the office, when they expect to be back, and with whom I can speak if I need a real, live human being.

48. Volunteer Together

Structure school projects, such as clean-up days, fun fairs, or concession booths at athletic events, in which teams of parents and teachers work together. There's nothing like a little hard work to build bonds of friendship.

49. What's in a Name?

Learn as many students' and parents' names as you can. After you've learned all of your students' names, learn something unique about each one. When you meet with a parent, hand out a compli-ment or two. Nothing will bring a smile to parents' faces faster than good news about their child.

50. Keep It up!

Send out an open-ended survey to parents. Use these three ques-tions to find out what your community is "really thinking":

- What are we currently doing that we should continue doing?
- What are we doing that we should stop doing?
- What aren't we doing that we should start doing?

References

A lesson on winking at abuse. (1996, November 26). *Chicago Tribune*, p. 16.

Argyris, C. (1986). Skilled incompetence. *Harvard Business Review, 64*, 74-79.

Argyris, C. (1990). *Overcoming organizational defenses*. Needham Heights, MA: Allyn & Bacon.

Argyris, C. (1991). Teaching smart people how to learn. *Harvard Business Review, 69*, 99-109.

Bailey, S. (1971). Preparing administrators for conflict resolution. *Educational Record, 53*, 225.

Berger, J. (1991, November 27). Matter-of-factly, New York City begins school condom program. *New York Times*, pp. A1, A9.

Bradley, A. (1997, March 26). Educated consumers. *Education Week*, pp. 33-34.

Brinkman, R., & Kirschner, R. (1994). *Dealing with people you can't stand*. New York: McGraw-Hill.

Brown, J., & Isaacs, D. (1994). *The fifth discipline fieldbook: Strategies and tools for building a learning organization*. Garden City, NY: Doubleday.

Class sees "Striptease." (1997, May 28). *Education Week*, p. 4.

Covey, S. (1989). *7 habits of highly effective people*. New York: Simon & Schuster.

Freeman, L. (1996, November 6). Talking to parents about school reform. *Education Week, 37*, p. 40.

Gay student wins discrimination case. (1996, November 21). *Milwaukee Journal-Sentinel*, p. 23.

Harrington, D., & Young, L. (1993). *School savvy: Everything you need to know to guide your child through today's schools*. New York: Noonday.

Keogh, J. (1996). *Getting the best education for your child*. Los Angeles: Lowell House.

Kipling, R. (1936). If. In H. Felleman (Ed.), *The best loved poems of the American people* (p. 65). Garden City, NY: Doubleday.

Lawsuits that target schools and teachers are part of new wave. (1996, November 11). *Arizona Daily Star*, p. B5.

Ledell, M., & Arnsparger, A. (1993). *How to deal with community criticism of school change.* Denver, CO: Education Commission of the States.

Leo, J. (1997, June 16). On society. *U.S. News and World Report*, p. 19.

Lindelow, J., & Mazzarella, J. A. (1983). School climate. In S. C. Smith, J. A. Mazzarella, & P. K. Piele (Eds.), *School leadership: Handbook for survival* (p. 169). Eugene, OR: Clearinghouse on Educational Management.

Lindsay, D. (1996, February 14). Telling tales out of school. *Education Week*, pp. 27-31.

Lynch, R. F., & Werner, T. J. (1992). *Continuous improvement: Teams and tools.* Atlanta, GA: QualTeam.

Mack, D. (1997). *The assault on parenthood: How our culture undermines the family.* New York: Simon & Schuster.

Matthews, D. (1996). *Is there a public for the public schools?* Dayton, OH: Kettering Foundation Press.

McEwan, E. K. (1992). *Solving school problems: Kindergarten through middle school.* Wheaton, IL: Harold Shaw.

McEwan, E. K. (1996a). *"The dog ate it." Conquering homework hassles.* Wheaton, IL: Harold Shaw.

McEwan, E. K. (1996b). *"I didn't do it." Dealing with dishonesty.* Wheaton, IL: Harold Shaw.

McEwan, E. K. (1996c). *"I hate school." What to do when your child won't go.* Wheaton, IL: Harold Shaw.

McEwan, E. K. (1996d). *"Nobody likes me." Helping your child make friends.* Wheaton, IL: Harold Shaw.

McEwan, E. K. (1997a). *Leading your team to excellence: How to make quality decisions.* Thousand Oaks, CA: Corwin Press.

McEwan, E. K. (1997b). *7 steps to effective instructional leadership.* Thousand Oaks, CA: Corwin Press.

Nemko, M., & Nemko, B. (1986). *How to get your child a private school education in a public school.* Washington, DC: Acropolis.

Olson, L. (1995, June 14). Cards on the table. *Education Week*, pp. 23-28.

Peck, M. S. (1978). *The road less traveled.* New York: Simon & Schuster.

Peck, M. S. (1983). *People of the lie.* New York: Simon & Schuster.

Portner, J. (1996, June 19). N.H. parents organized to take aim at discipline. *Education Week*, p. 10.

Riechmann, D. (1996, October 7). Critics give schools PC rating for strict adherence to rules. *Boston Globe*, p. A4.

Roberts, C. (1994). What you can expect from team learning. In P. Senge, A. Kleiner, C. Roberts, R. B. Ross, & B. J. Smith (Eds.), *The fifth discipline fieldbook: Strategies and tools for building a learning organization* (pp. 353-357). Garden City, NY: Doubleday.

Schein, E. (1992). *Organizational culture and leadership.* San Francisco: Jossey-Bass.

Senge, P. (1990). *The fifth discipline.* Garden City, NY: Doubleday.

Senge, P., Kleiner, A., Roberts, C., Ross, R. B., & Smith, B. J. (Eds.). (1994). *The fifth discipline fieldbook: Strategies and tools for building a learning organization.* Garden City, NY: Doubleday.

Steinke, P. L. (1996). *Healthy congregations: A systems approach.* Washington, DC: Alban Institute.

Tavris, C. (1978). *Anger: The misunderstood emotion.* New York: Simon & Schuster.

Teacher pens note on face. (1997, November 27). *Education Week,* p. 4.

Toch, T., with Gest, T., & Guttman, M. (1993, November 8). Violence in schools. *U.S. News and World Report,* pp. 30-37.

Vest, J. (1997, May 26). Do school counselors subvert children? *U.S. News and World Report,* p. 25.

Walsh, M. (1996, November 17). Confidential agreement in Berkeley sex-abuse case sparks criticism. *Education Week,* p. 9.

White, K. A. (1996, November 13). Colorado voters reject parent-rights measure. *Education Week,* p. 1.

Wegela, K. K. (1996). *How to be a help instead of a nuisance.* Boston: Shambhala.

Zey, M.G. (1990). *Winning with people: Building lifelong professional and personal success through the supporting cast principle.* Los Angeles: Jeremy P. Tarcher.

Index